TRACY EISNAUGLE

D1217340

MOVING TO SARASOTA

THE UN-TOURIST GUIDE

SECOND EDITION

CONTENTS

Moving to Sarasota   5
Foreword

Introduction   9
14 Reasons to Call Sarasota Home   11

Chapter 1   21
A Brief History of Sarasota
From Pre-History to the Early 1800s   21
Early 20th Century—The Ringlings and More   24
World War II and Renewed Growth   27
Post- World War II Population Explosion   28

Chapter 2   29
A Quick Geographic and Community Guide to Sarasota
Getting to Know Sarasota Communities   31
Getting Around Town   42

Chapter 3   45
The Climate and the Environment
Hurricane information   48

Chapter 4   51
Living Well in Sarasota
Cost of Living   51
Services   57

Chapter 5   66
Choosing Where to Live
Renting vs. Buying on the Suncoast   72
Shopping   74

Chapter 6   83
Never a Shortage of Things to Do
    Dining on the Suncoast   88
    Summer Nights All Year Long   91
    Getting Fit on the Suncoast   101

Chapter 7   107
Bringing Up Baby & Beyond—Pre-K to MBA
    Get Involved in the Community   122
    The Foundation of Community   123
    The Suncoast Social and Volunteer Scene   124

Chapter 8   129
Practical Notebook on Moving
    Transportation & Logistics   131

Chapter 9   133
The Economy on the Rebound

Conclusion   142

Acknowledgments   144

Author Biography   147

Key Resources: Websites and Phone Numbers   148

MOVING TO SARASOTA
FOREWORD

Writing to her husband of Sarasota's charms in the 1910s, Davie Lindsay Worcester told him, "This is what I want for my old age... Oh! Words cannot paint the scene imagination cannot conceive of such grandeur."

Such was Sarasota's inviting tropical beauty, augmented by climate that was described as "salubrious," beaches which were pristine, fishing and hunting that were unparalleled, a bay that was one of the most beautiful in the world, all combining to draw the first tourists to spend their winters here.

These ingredients were not enough though. Sarasota was still difficult to reach and offered little in the way of creature comforts; the small community was still primarily a fishing/agriculture backwater.

That would change with the mid-20s real estate boom. Within a handful of years, all the essentials for a bona fide city fell into place: housing developments, banks, hotels, bridges to the out islands, schools, paved streets, theatres, restaurants, public buildings, et. al. Everywhere one cared to look, construction was underway. We were billing ourselves at the Land of Glorified Opportunity. As one member of the burgeoning community put it, "Sarasota was electric with excitement."

The real estate bust in September of 1926, followed by the Great Depression and World War II put the good times on hold; but only temporarily. Post World War II growth rejuvenated Sarasota.

Sarasota's natural assets were augmented with cultural elements that would do proud cities many times larger.

Known as a cultural hub of the Gulf Coast ever since John Ringling built the John and Mable Ringling Museum of Art which he donated to the state along with his magnificent Ca' d'Zan (House of John), Sarasota also offers the Players Theatre, The Historic Asolo Theatre, the Van Wezel Performing Arts Hall which brings an eclectic array of world class talent, the magnificent Sarasota Opera, the Sarasota Ballet, Ringling School of Art and Design, numerous downtown art galleries, several noteworthy colleges including highly rated New College, University of South Florida, and the State College of Florida. The list is long.

Sarasota's downtown is unique and inviting. Located just a few steps from beautiful Sarasota Bay, it is filled with ethnic restaurants of all persuasions, galleries, boutiques, high-end condominiums, a well-stocked library, comfortable parks, and it still manages to retain many historic pieces of its past.

Sarasota's beaches are among the most beautiful in the world; blindingly white sand contrasting with the multi-hued azure colors of the Gulf of Mexico. Siesta Beach was recently singled out as the most beautiful beach in the world by Dr. Beach.

Another unique feature of Sarasota is St. Armand's Circle and the people friendly Ringling Bridge leading to it. Always filled with walkers, runners, and bicyclists the bridge has become a focal point for local exercisers. The Circle with its upscale shops and restaurants fulfills John Ringling's dream of a tropical utopia.

Taken all together, Sarasota is unequalled.

Courtesy of: Jeff LaHurd

Local author/historian Jeff LaHurd has lived in Sarasota since 1950 and has written 15 books about the history of the community plus numerous articles. Jeff is a former board member of the Sarasota Alliance for Historic Preservation, the Sarasota Historical Society, the Sarasota Community Blood Bank, and the

Downtown Kiwanis Club. He is currently a member of the Friends of the Sarasota County History Center. He and his wife Jennifer have four children. He is employed at the Sarasota County Department of Historical Resources as a History Specialist.

INTRODUCTION

Congratulations. If you have purchased this book, you have either decided to move to Sarasota or are seriously considering a move to our beautiful Gulf Coast city. In either case, my goal is to provide all the information you need to assist in making Sarasota your new home. I would like to officially welcome you to The Suncoast and hope that you fall as much in love with this tropical paradise as I have. You'll find it hard to imagine living anywhere else once you're settled into our small, sophisticated city. I want to make it easy for you and your family to feel truly welcome as a new Sarasota resident.

Courtesy of: Detlev von Kessel - pix360

Not Just for Tourists and Retirees

Yes, Sarasota is home to many snowbirds and seniors, but our pristine beaches and warm Gulf waters attract families and the young alike.

Most of you started your love affair with our tropical oasis as carefree vacationers soaking up the sun and relaxing on the beach. Our typical transplants began with an enjoyable stay in our area and kept returning until the day their love affair for our city took hold. Then, with a leap of faith, they decided to move here either part or full time.

Sarasota is a melting pot of people from all over the world. On any given day, as you walk the downtown streets or the coastal shoreline, you will hear a vast array of accents and languages. The appeal of the Suncoast brings a wonderful mix of people creating a relaxed, open, and inviting atmosphere.

Welcome to Sarasota!

Courtesy of: CMS Photography

14 Reasons to Call Sarasota Home

Reason #1
Sarasota is Actually Affordable

Because residents benefit from no state income tax, low property taxes, a variety of budget-friendly housing options, and low energy costs, Sarasota can be a very affordable place to live. Compared to larger cities like Boston, New York City, Chicago or Washington D.C. the cost of living in Sarasota is a bargain. If you elect to make Florida your permanent state of residence you will also qualify for the Homestead Exemption which results in an extra annual $25,000 property tax deduction.

Reason #2
Winterless Wonderland

Yes, it is hot and humid in the summer, but no hotter than a typical August day in Washington, DC. Happily, we live along the coastline that blesses us with a daily refreshing Gulf breeze and frequent afternoon rain showers that offer relief from the heat.

Courtesy of: CMS Photography

The reward for making it through the summer heat is the promise of no snow. So, trade in your scary tire chains, noisy snow blowers, ugly mittens, and sloppy galoshes for some much needed sunblock, swimsuits, sporty convertibles, and flip flops.

Reason #3
Cultural Mecca

No matter what cultural and arts activities you enjoy, Sarasota has something for you year-round. Of course, the October thru May season in Sarasota offers the richest array of activities that include elegant Galas and Charity events, unforgettable Opera performances, a host of theatre options, musical entertainment, art walks and gallery showcases, a ten-day film festival, sand sculpting competition, and much, much more. Check out the Thursday Ticket in the Sarasota Herald Tribune as well as the multitude of social calendars available on line.

Courtesy of: Sarasota Opera

Reason #4
Award Winning White Sand Beaches

In 2011 <u>Dr. Beach</u>, a.k.a. Dr. Stephen P. Leatherman, yes he is a real doctor and director of FIU's highly respected Laboratory for Coastal Research, and considered America's Foremost Beach Expert awarded Siesta Key as America's Best Beach. The Intracoastal Waterway flows along the east side of the Key with the Gulf along the west. Siesta Beach is renowned for its brilliantly white sugar fine crystal sand that consists of 99% pure quartz, keeping it magically cool under your feet. In addition to Siesta Beach, you can enjoy the sun and sand on Longboat Key, Lido with its public pool, Crescent, Turtle, Nokomis, and Venice beaches. All are free to the public.

Courtesy of: Robert Pope Photography

Reason #5
Multiple Housing Options

Courtesy of: Robert Pope Photography

Greater Sarasota offers a vast array of housing options -- from villas to townhomes, to condominiums, to humble historic houses, to mansions, to large acreage estates. Whatever your heart desires, the Suncoast has it. A four bedroom, three bath home with a refreshing pool, located in Palmer Ranch is currently priced at approximately $500,000, while a beachfront two bedroom, two bath condominium on Lido Key would cost around $600,000 and a single family home on 3 acres in Northport is priced just under $400,000.

Reason #6
Best Place to Retire...

You may be reading this book because you are considering Sarasota as your retirement home. If so, you're in agreement with the experts. In fact, Money Magazine ranks Sarasota 7th for "Top Places to Retire Young" as well as the "Nation's Best Small City" and one of the "Best Places to Retire".

The article credits Sarasota for having, "the most splendid architecture anywhere in the Sunshine State. It also boasts pure white sands, exotic birds and plants, boating, water skiing, opera, and ballets."

Reason #7
Excellent Healthcare...

Our four local hospital facilities provide exceptional healthcare services throughout the region, as numerous awards prove. Money Magazine rated Sarasota as one of the "Best Cities with the Best Healthcare Systems" and Sarasota Memorial Health Care System was rated within the "America's 50 Best Hospitals" by U.S. News & World Report as well as "10 of the Largest Safe Hospitals in the U.S." by Forbes.com.

Reason #8
Flourishing Business Climate...

We're open for business. Forbes ranks Sarasota 11th in "Best Cities for Jobs". Sarasota County consists of more than 20,000 businesses, of which 75 percent are considered small to medium size companies with fewer than 25 employees.

According to the U.S. Bureau of Labor Statistics, Sarasota's unemployment rate in April, 2015 was 4.2 percent. That's an impressive recovery from the 2010 unemployment rate of 11.9 percent and the 2013 rate of 6.7 percent. The Greater Sarasota Chamber of Commerce, The Economic Development Corporation, as well as the The HuB counsel entrepreneurs in developing new ideas and creating new businesses in our area. Since its inception in 2009, the HuB has supported over two-hundred entrepreneurs, launched twenty businesses and twelve major campaigns to support creative change on the Suncoast.

Reason #9
Fantastic for Foodies...

When it comes to great food, Sarasota delivers. Sarasota is home to more than fourteen hundred restaurants from elegant gourmet eateries to fantastic food trucks. No matter what you crave, you can find it or find the fixings to prepare it. We have multiple fresh food markets, boutique/specialty grocery stores, weekly farmer's markets, traditional butcher shops, fresh seafood vendors (of course) and Amish stores and restaurants.

Courtesy of: Duval's New World Café

Reason #10
An Abundance of High Quality Education Opportunities

We do a superb job educating our children. Our county has a higher percentage of high school graduates than the state of Florida and the nation. Over 90% of Sarasota County high school seniors graduate. Our dropout rate is just 2%.

Sarasota County has a variety of education options for children and adults from traditional public schools, to charter schools, private and Montessori settings, adult education facilities, technical and specialty schools as well as universities. Almost 30% of Sarasota residents have earned a bachelor's degree with science and engineering topping the field of study.

Reason #11
Parks and Wildlife

It's easy and fun to enjoy native wildlife in greater Sarasota whether you love bird watching, hiking, observing alligators or swimming with the fishes. We have over 120 parks and trails encompassing over 3,000 acres. Among our favorites is the ever-expanding Legacy Trail whose recreational walking and biking trail stretches over ten miles along the former CSX Railroad corridor. Another terrific outdoor experience is the venerable Myakka State Park, once part of Bertha Palmer's ranch. Its 60 square miles make it one of the largest parks in the state.

Reason #12
The Greatest Show on Earth—and More

The circus goes way back to the 1920s in Sarasota history, when The Ringlings joined the Florida land boom and selected Sarasota as their winter residence. Ever since, we've been blessed with generations of circus performers making Sarasota their home. In 1949 a small high school gymnastics class evolved into the Sailor Circus, a youth training program for students 4th to 12th grades, which is still an active student program. Their newly renovated facility is just south of the Sarasota High School Campus. The Sailor Circus is now part of Circus Sarasota.

Don't think you've lost your mind if you hear the roars of the big cats while traveling out east or visiting the celery fields. You've just found The Big Cat Habitat and Gulf Coast Sanctuary, a non-profit safe haven for a menagerie of rescued exotic wildlife cared for by Kay Rosarie who comes from a rich circus heritage. The famous wirewalker Nik Wallenda also calls Sarasota home.

Courtesy of: Richard Czina

Reason #13
Amish & Mennonite Population

Many people are astonished when they discover Sarasota's flourishing Amish and Mennonite communities. Usually it occurs while driving down Bahia Vista Street and happening upon a cluster of bearded men and bonnet-capped women riding their three-wheel bicycles. We have been attracting Amish and Mennonite residents since the early 1920's.

Although they were originally attracted to the area for winter farming, many stayed as year-round residents, establishing churches, farmland, and local businesses that still thrive in the area today.

Reason #14
Endless Supply of Things to Do:

Sarasotans are never at a loss for something to do. Here's just a tiny sampling of your options:

- Head to the ballpark and catch a Baltimore Orioles spring training game.

- Kayak through the mangroves surrounding our extensive coastline.

- Sip and savor the sunset on a booze cruise.

- Get your toes in the sand at a Summer Siesta Beach Run.

- View the masters at The Ringling Museum of Art.

- Learn about our marine life at Mote Marine Aquarium.

- Step back in time with a Sarasota History Alive tour.

- Kick off your shoes and enjoy a free concert at Van Wezel's Friday Fest.

- Have a beer or glass of wine while enjoying a film at Burns Court Cinema.

- Shop till you drop and dine toll you pop at St. Armand's Circle or the new Mall at UTC...

CHAPTER 1

A BRIEF HISTORY OF SARASOTA

From Pre-History to the Early 1800s

Tranquil Sarasota Bay has been attracting inhabitants since the ice thawed and the water retreated to reveal its brilliant coastline and pristine waters. As it evolved into a flourishing coastal ecosystem with bountiful fishing, this inviting living environment was home to the Paleo-Indian tribes residing along the west coast of Florida dating back to 8,000 BC. Maps from the mid-eighteen century recognize the area as Zarazote, thought to be a name given to the region by the original native-American tribes including the Seminole, Tocobaga and Caloosa.

In the 1500s the first Spanish explorers Ponce de Leon, Panfilo Narvaez and Hernando De Soto landed on the Gulf coast in search of silver and gold only to discover a fisherman's paradise. They established trading camps or ranchos which thrived along the bayfront. The Spanish took advantage of the rich bay waters providing excellent fishing and marine trade. The area changed hands between the Spanish and English multiple times over the next few hundred years.

In 1819, the United States acquired Florida as a territory. It became a state in 1821. The 1842 Armed Occupation Act allowed for private ownership of land along Sarasota Bay, but only for incoming settlers. The native Seminoles and other tribes were not allowed to become citizens or to own land and were pushed even further to the south, eventually many of them fled Florida entirely. In 1845 the United

States army established Fort Armistead along Sarasota Bay and the European settlers began arriving in substantial numbers. Over time, the city's name evolved into Sara Sota. In 1845 Sarasota was designated as part of Hillsborough County and became part of Manatee County ten years later.

Courtesy of: Sarasota County Department of Historical Resources

The significant achievements of our early 19th century settlers are still evident and appreciated today. In 1843, William Whitaker was the first documented pioneer arriving in Sarasota. In 1867, the Webb family came to Sarasota from Utica, New York and settled in the Spanish Point area which is now considered Osprey. In 1885, the Browning family attempted to create a Scottish Colony by launching a large campaign promoting Sarasota as a waterfront paradise to the residents of Scotland.

Col. John Hamilton Gillespie was sent over from Scotland after the original colony failed to revive the effort. Gillespie began to develop Sarasota. In 1887 Gillespie built the De Sota Hotel and in 1886 he completed a two hole golf course which is thought to be one of the first golf courses in America. By 1905 he had completed a 110-acre nine-hole course.

Courtesy of: Sarasota County Department of Historical Resources

**Courtesy of: Sarasota County Department of Historical Resources
– Lillian Burns Collection**

Early 20ᵗʰ Century—The Ringlings and More

The village of Sarasota was incorporated for local government as a town under state guidelines in 1902 with John Hamilton Gillespie as the town's first mayor. It was re-platted in 1912 and its government then was incorporated as a city in 1913 with A.B. Edwards as mayor. In 1921, Sarasota was separated from Manatee and established as its own county.

Owen Burns settled in Sarasota only to become the largest landowner in the city with holdings that included all of Lido Key. He founded a bank, constructed landmark buildings and mansions, and built the original John Ringling Causeway. Burns also dredged the harbor and created the new bay front point with reclaimed soil. The Burns Court area and Cinema are still thriving within the city today. Owen Burns also went into business with John Ringling to develop the barrier islands.

Courtesy of: Sarasota County Department of Historical Resources

The families of John Ringling and Charles Ringling settled along the northern Sarasota bayfront in the early 1920's. The Ringling Brothers

Circus established its winter home in Sarasota during 1927, resulting in performers and staff members also settling in the area. The circus influence can be seen throughout our area with the Sarasota High School's Sailor Circus, Circus Sarasota, the Ringling's Clown College and Circus museums. Sarasota truly is the "Circus Capital of the World."

After World War I, Sarasota experienced an economic boom. Charles Ringling invested inland, developed property, founded a bank, and built the Sarasota Terrace Hotel. Their home, the Edith Ringling Estate, is now the center of the New College of Florida campus.

John Ringling, in partnership with Owen Burns, developed the barrier islands including Lido Key and St. Armand Key. They also dredged land to create Golden Gate Point. To facilitate the development, they built a bridge to the islands which is currently named the John Ringling Causeway. Because the Ringling home known as the Ca'D'Zan and Museum are open to the public, you can still experience the opulence of the era today.

Courtesy of: Sarasota County Department of Historical Resources

Women also had a role in Sarasota's building and land development. In 1913 two sisters, Katherine McClellan and Daisietta McClellan, became real estate developers and created the McClellan Park subdivision. Bertha Honore Palmer from Chicago became the region's largest landholder, rancher and developer at the start of the twentieth century, when she purchased 90,000 acres of property. Two large areas of her estate were granted back to the government as parks including what is now Historic Spanish Point and Myakka State Park. She also purchased and resided on the Webb estate on Historic Spanish Point, which is listed on the National Register of Historic Places and open to the public.

Street Scene - Pinecraft, Fla.   2-1-608

Bahia Vista St., Looking East   1952

Courtesy of: Sarasota County Department of Historical Resources

In 1925, the Amish and Mennonite societies from Ohio and Pennsylvania began to settle in Sarasota looking for warm weather and the ability to farm during the winter months. Their first community was the Sarasota National Tourist Camp which included 454 lots each measuring 40 by 40 feet. In 1926, Earl S. and Mary K. Craft platted the Pinecraft neighborhood with additional lots running east and west of Phillippi Creek. The Amish and Mennonite settlers have built business centers, communities and places of worship throughout the area. But, Pinecraft remains the heart of their community.

World War II and Renewed Growth

As the great depression came in the 1930s, the Florida land boom cratered and growth came to a halt until World War II. During the war, the United States Army selected Florida as an ideal location for flight training with its flat, open terrain and favorable weather. By 1942, two Army air stations were open and operating in Sarasota County including the Sarasota Army Airfield for bomber pilot training which transitioned into a fighter station later that same year and the Venice Air Base established as a training school for fighter pilots. Over the course of the war, more than 6,000 military personnel were stationed at the two locations. Soon after the war ended, both bases were deactivated and turned over to the local governments. Both locations are still active airport facilities today.

One of the most significant trends of the post-war era in Florida has been a steady growth in population. This trend resulted from large migrations from other areas within the U.S. as well as from countries around the world, notably China and Haiti. Florida is now the fourth most populous state in the nation.

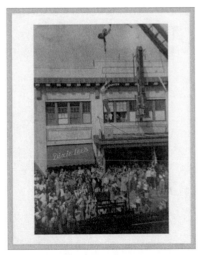

Since World War II, Florida's economy also has become more diverse. Tourism, cattle, citrus, and phosphate have been joined by a host of new industries that have greatly expanded the numbers of jobs available to residents. Electronics, plastics, construction, real estate, and international banking are among the state's more recently-developed industries.

Courtesy of: Sarasota County Department of Historical Resources

Post-World War II Population Explosion

During the post-war years, Sarasota County experienced a population explosion. The 19,000 residents in 1945 grew to 120,413 in 1970. Part of the explosion occurred within the arts community. A significant number of artists, writers, and architects moved to the area and art, theatre, and musical groups emerged. Jungle Gardens, Sunshine Springs and Gardens, Circus Hall of Fame, Floridaland, and Texas Jim Mitchell's Reptile Farm and Zoo opened to entice the Florida-bound traveler. The Ringling circus winter quarters moved to Venice and its Sarasota site became a subdivision. Baseball spring training continued with the Chicago White Sox, the Cincinnati Reds, and now the Baltimore Orioles.

Although Sarasota suffered badly in the 2008 real estate collapse that hit the entire country, it has now bounced back and returned to a more gentle upward growth curve.

Our warm waters and healthy climate have again renewed their attraction for the wealthy, for young families, for retirees, for artists seeking inspiration, for the Amish and Mennonite colonies, and, of course, for the circus folk.

***Excerpts above from:
Sarasota County Design Guidelines for Historic Properties

CHAPTER 2
A QUICK GEOGRAPHIC AND COMMUNITY GUIDE TO SARASOTA

Sarasota is both a county and a city, which is only slightly confusing when it comes to voting and garbage pickup.

The City of Sarasota, which lies within the county, is only 25.9 square miles of which 14.9 square miles is land and 11.0 square miles is water. The overall county including the city area encompasses over 563 square miles surrounded by 37 miles of pristine Gulf of Mexico shoreline.

The Sarasota County area includes the cities of Sarasota, Venice, North Port and the Town of Longboat Key. There are four main residential barrier islands or keys including Siesta Key, Lido Key, Longboat Key and Casey Key. Residents also refer to different locations by their regional name such as Myakka, Palmer Ranch, Osprey and Nokomis, just to name a few.

The County's population fluctuates seasonally expanding from approximately 390,000 permanent residents to more than 476,000 during the winter months. For the purpose of this book, we are excluding some of the rural outlying eastern or southern communities that border on Manatee, De Soto and Charlotte Counties as well as the Lakewood Ranch community as the residential section of Lakewood Ranch is primarily in Manatee County.

Sarasota includes multiple thoroughfares. The main north-to-south options are:

- US41 also known as the Tamiami Trail

- Interstate 75

- Honore Avenue, which is currently being widened to provide much needed traffic relief to the interstate system

- Beneva Road

- Tuttle Avenue which turns into Swift also runs N-S but doesn't traverse the full length of county

Traveling east-to-west has a multitude of options. Every I75 exit leads to roads that run E-W across the county connecting US41 to I75 creating a grid that will get you where you need to go. These include: Fruitville Road, Bee Ridge Road, Clark Road, Laurel Road and Jacaranda Boulevard. A good rule of thumb is "East = Interstate, West = Water".

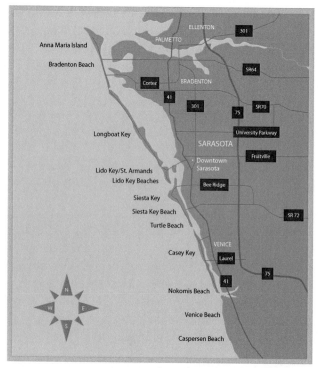

Courtesy of: Reid Gerletti

Getting to Know Sarasota Communities

Downtown Sarasota

This area of Sarasota is centered around Main Street which starts near US 301 and ends at Bayfront Park. It comprises multiple small surrounding communities most of which are located with the city limits.

The city of Sarasota is home to approximately 55,000 residents. The downtown area is a great place to live because it offers a walkable community lifestyle. This densely populated area combines both commercial and residential environments that include high rise and mid-rise buildings, as well as single family homes tucked along charming perimeter neighborhoods.

A three bedroom, 2 bathroom condominium downtown will cost between $500,000-$700,000 depending on the building amenities and view. Some of the luxurious waterfront condominiums cost in excess of $3,000,000. While a three bedroom, 2 bath single-family home will cost between $525,000 - $1,000,000 depending on the community. The neighborhoods north of Fruitville Road, Gillespie Park and the Rosemary District are considered to be in transition and home prices are still lower. But, as these communities see an influx of end user purchasers, their prices will begin to rise. These urban communities are just a short stroll to all of downtown amenities, including a Whole Foods, hundreds of restaurants, Selby Library, multiple theatres and entertainment, parks and recreational facilities including City Island Park and Selby Gardens.

Courtesy of: Detlev von Kessel - pix360

Northern Sarasota/ The Museum Area

Appropriately called the Museum area because of its proximity to the Ringling, this eclectic collection of neighborhoods sits along the Sarasota Bayfront and showcases some of the area's most spectacular views of Sarasota Bay and Longboat Key.

Historic Ringling era homes are nestled among newer replicas and modern marvels creating a whimsical and enchanting environment surrounded by ancient oaks and tropical wildlife. The captivating neighborhoods of Sapphire Shores, Indian Beach and Whitfield Estates reside in this area and offer a wide selection of single-family homes starting in the $600,000 price range and going all the way up to the $5,000,000 mansions. One of the highest priced residential home sales set a record in 2015 at $10,000,000 in this area.

Ringling College of Art + Design and New College of Florida as well as Sarasota Bradenton International Airport grace the northern section of the county. As you travel east along the northern border, the neighborhoods offer a variety of housing options and the convenience of nearby amenities that include shopping, dining and a movie theatre stretching far east to the Sarasota side of Lakewood Ranch and Sarasota Polo Club.

Central Sarasota

The diverse heart of Sarasota extends from centrally located Bee Ridge Road north to Fruitville Road and south to Clark Road—and west of Interstate 75 extending to US 41. Central Sarasota has so many different neighborhoods and housing options that there is truly something for everyone. New communities mix with older ones to create a nice balance of pricing and housing styles. Convenient, intermingled commercial development offers ease of access for residents to markets, services and entertainment options. Prices for homes will vary depending on the neighborhood, amenities, square footage, acreage, view and proximity to any type of water or golf course; $275,000 will buy a nice three bedroom, 2 bath, pool home in the Forest Lakes neighborhood, while $350,000 will buy a comparable home in the community of The Lakes.

West of the Trail

Historic charm and eclectic grace lure people to this enchanting part of town where new Mediterranean inspired and stunning modern residences blend with timeless antique homes to create an attractively diverse community. Appropriately named for its location, it includes neighborhoods west of Tamiami Trail from Mound Street to Stickney Point Road, including Harbor Acres, McClellan Park, the flower named streets, Cherokee Park and Oyster Bay just to name a few. The homes in these coveted neighborhoods hold their value. Recent recorded sales range in price from $400,000 to the highest recorded sale for far for 2015 which was $6,825,000. The average sales price for a four bedroom, three bath home with a pool is approximately $900,000. A record sale was recorded in July of 2015 within this area closing at $6,825,000, which is the second highest price paid for a single-family home in Sarasota, Manatee and Charlotte County in 2015.

The average sales price for a four bedroom, three bath home with a pool is currently $882,000. Proximity to Sarasota Memorial Hospital and to the Southside Shopping Village makes for both a practical and a picturesque community.

Palmer Ranch

This beautiful master-planned community sits on over 10,000 acres just south of Clark Road. Palmer Ranch is just minutes to Siesta Key and home to the Westfield Shopping Mall with new AMC movie theatre and Costco, many shopping centers offering a variety of dining and specialty stores, as well as multiple golf courses, the Legacy Trail, and a large family YMCA with the Selby Aquatic Center.

The Palmer Ranch community includes twenty-three neighborhoods that offer residents a variety of housing options from apartment living, condominiums, villas, townhomes, single-family homes, and assisted living environments. The variety of communities and amenities reflect a large range in pricing. The current price for a two bedroom, two bath condominium ranges from $125,000 to $300,000, while a three bedroom, two bathroom villa has a price range from $145,000 to $450,000 and a three bedroom, two bathroom single-family pool home will cost between $425,000 to $700,000. This vast community is surrounded by white decorative fencing and consistent signage at the multiple entrances, some of Bertha Palmer's original farmland still remains untouched. And, the sight of grazing cattle evokes a nice reminder of our humble past.

Osprey & Nokomis

Tucked along the southwestern region of central Sarasota, these smaller communities include a variety of neighborhoods such as the exclusive Country Club of The Oaks and multiple Sorrento enclaves. Close to the Venice jetties, these waterfront areas are a mariner's paradise, providing swift boating access to the Gulf of Mexico and the Intracoastal Waterway, as well as the tranquil waters of Roberts Bay and Dona Bay.

Homes in the Sorrento neighborhoods range in price from $195,000 to over $1,000,000, while homes behind the gates of The Oaks range from $600,000 to close to $3,000,000. Just south of the intersection on Beneva Road and Tamiami Trail these communities are just a quick drive to all that central Sarasota and Venice have to offer with their own charm and attractions including Historic Spanish Point and Oscar Scherer State Park.

Courtesy of: Detlev von Kessel - pix360

Venice

The City of Venice, in southern Sarasota County, contains a total area of 16.6 square miles of land and 1.4 square miles of water. Venice hosts an annual Shark's Tooth Festival celebrating the plethora of sharks teeth found along the legendary shoreline.

Seven miles of pristine beaches have helped Venice to attract a year-round population of 20,748 and many more seasonal residents. A single-family, three bedroom, two-bathroom pool home in Venice ranges in price from $215,000 to over $4,000,000 so the variety and selection are endless. Its thriving historic downtown district is known as "The Island of Venice." Residents enjoy the cultural arts scene with art festivals throughout the year.

East County & Myakka

Sarasota continues to grow east of Interstate 75 as the areas closest to the waterfront are largely built out. Sprawling new communities in the east county area offer residents upscale gated neighborhoods such as The Forest at Hi Hat Ranch off Clark Road. Popular golf course communities include the Audubon rated golf course at The Venetian located off Laurel Road in Venice and The Founders Club off Fruitville Road.

The Myakka area itself is a rural community offering large tracts of land for pastoral living, farming and livestock. Single-family homes on expansive one-acre home sites in the Oak Ford Golf Club community are currently selling for $375,000 to $500,000. The Polo Club on the southern side of University Parkway caters to Polo enthusiasts who require stables for their polo ponies. Hidden River is one of the very few Gulf Coast aviation communities which offers residents access to the neighborhood's private 2600 foot air strip. Hidden River permits residents to park aircraft and have airplane hangars on their personal property. Lot sizes, home styles and prices range from $300,000 to over $1,000,000

North Port

Tucked along the southern most section of the county The City of North Port encompasses a total area of 74.8 square miles of land and 0.8 square miles of water. North Port is the newest city in the county with a median resident age of only 38, making it the youngest in Southwest Florida. The population of North Port was 57,357 in 2010 and continues to grow. The Census Bureau estimated the 2013 population to be 59,212 residents.

North Port is known for its natural springs and more than 80 miles of freshwater canals. Housing in this area is very affordable because of its greater distance from central Sarasota county amenities. The average single family, three bedroom, two-bath home with a pool costs just $165,000.

The Barrier Islands
Lido Key, Bird Key & St. Armand's Circle

The Ringling Causeway connects to these water-surrounded communities which showcase resort style living at its finest. The brilliantly renovated Sarasota Yacht Club sits at the entrance to Lido Key benefiting from deep water and boating accessibility. Exclusive Bird Key offers multiple housing options from direct waterfront

Courtesy of: Detlev von Kessel - pix360

to canal and garden site locations; their private yacht club serves residents. St. Armand's Key has a land area of 83.6 acres and is home to the renowned St. Armand's Circle. Serving as the area hub, this charming shopping and dining destination attracts tourists and residents year-round.

Lido Key encompasses 530 acres with a long stretch of public beach with coveted white powder sand but lacks lifeguards. There is also a concession area and public pool. Lido is home to both high rise and mid-rise condominiums including the Ritz Carlton Beach Residences as well as single family homes. On the south side of Lido is a serene nature preserve area with a public park and beach with lifeguards on duty during weekends during the summer. Single-family, three bedroom, two bath homes in this area cost between $700,000 to $3,000,000, while a beachfront, two bedroom, two bath condominium costs from $350,000 to $1,000,000 depending on the view.

Courtesy of: Detlev von Kessel - pix360

Longboat Key

Longboat Key is a 10.8-mile long barrier island that lies in both Sarasota and Manatee Counties. Home to 8,000 full-time residents and 12,000 seasonal residents, Longboat Key contains 6,058 condominiums and 1,778 single-family homes. Longboat Key housing costs vary depending on location, either bayside or Gulf side as well as the neighborhood, amenities and view. A three bedroom, two-bath condominium can range in price from $429,000 to $2,275,000, while a similar in size single-family home ranges in price from $600,000 to over $2,000,000. Beyond the beaches and nature parks, Longboat is home to the Longboat Key Club & Resort.

Courtesy of: Detlev von Kessel - pix360

Siesta Key

Two drawbridges connect this spectacular 8-mile barrier island to the mainland. Siesta Drive leads to the north bridge while Stickney Point gives way to the south bridge providing dual access.

This small yet remarkable island has four main areas: The Village which is a central shopping, dining and entertainment area, Siesta Beach itself, Crescent Beach which is just off the south bridge with beach access, shopping and dining, and Turtle Beach which is the southernmost beach with public boat launch and campsite.

Both single family homes and condominiums are available bayside on the Intracoastal Waterway, on waterfront canal sites, internal island homes with canal access or no water frontage, and Gulf side beach residences. Single-family three bedroom, two bathroom homes start at $475,000 to over $1,000,000, while the prices for a two bedroom, two bath condominiums have the largest range from $195,000 to $950,000 with options to meet everyone's budget.

Courtesy of: Detlev von Kessel - pix360

Casey Key

The Blackburn Point one-lane swing bridge built in 1925 leads to a single meandering road along this narrow enclave of private estates. Casey Key, with no commercial buildings, large-scale condominiums or stop lights maintains a quaint and unique exclusivity. This 8 mile long barrier island is home to close to 400 residents and spectacular Gulf to Bay estates.. Casey Key homes are all priced over $1,000,000. Many famous celebrities reside on Casey Key, including author Stephen King.

Getting Around Town

Sarasota is a large county with a bustling population. Happily, the area's shopping centers, grocery stores, restaurants, and public facilities are well distributed throughout the region. Unfortunately, we lack a comprehensive mass transit system. Downtown Sarasota provides residents with a walkable/bikeable community, but most other county residents will need a car to get around town with ease.

For non-drivers, Sarasota County does provide a public bus system, SCAT (Sarasota County Area Transit), offering multiple fixed-routes that run Monday thru Saturday with limited itineraries available on Sunday. The SCAT routes and schedule maps are located online and available at the Downtown Transfer Station, Transit Administration building on Pinkney Avenue, Robert L. Anderson County Administration Center in Venice, North Port City Hall and Goodwill Store locations. SCAT also offers a Plus Service/Accessible Transportation to assist individuals with disabilities. For south county residents the SCAT system provides North Port Park & Ride service for commuters. SCAT offers multiple fare plans in addition to discounts for senior citizens, Medicare users and students.

Many private taxi/car services are available in Sarasota County. New to the area is Jonnys Free Beach Rides, which provides free (drivers do accept tips) transportation that is fun, safe and eco-friendly on Siesta Key.

Downtown has numerous parking options with over 4000 public parking spaces. A beautiful new parking garage on Palm Avenue downtown offers a low cost public option but does not allow overnight parking. We have free street parking downtown with time limits from 30 minutes to 3 hours. Our legendary beaches also offer parking, but you'll need a very early start on weekends and holidays.

Getting Out of Town

The <u>Sarasota Bradenton International</u> Airport, SRQ serving over one million travelers each year makes flying a breeze. This conveniently accessible airport is small, personable and easy to navigate. American, Delta, JetBlue, U.S. Airways, United and Air Canada all serve the airport, with non-stop service to many popular destinations. The beautifully maintained airport contains meeting rooms, shopping, dining options, and rental car assistance.

CHAPTER 3

THE CLIMATE AND THE ENVIRONMENT

Sarasota Seasons and Weather

We enjoy a humid subtropical climate with hot, damp summers and mild to cool winters. Our summer humidity takes some getting used to. But, I truly believe our dewy salt saturated air is nature's anti-aging remedy keeping us youthful and active. Humidity's positive impact on our skin and joints are fantastic. Our hot wet summers are more than balanced by our sunny, mild, and dry winters. Because we maintain a touch of tropical moisture during the winter you don't need to apply chapstick constantly. We experience a June to September rainy season and an October to May dry season. Although our temperatures adjust with the typical calendar seasons, the range is slight and change is gradual. The average annual air temperature is 72.6 F (22.6 C), while the average annual high is 82.8 F (28.2 C) and the average annual low temperature is 62.9 F (17.2 C). Of course, the heat index, (the combination of air temperature and humidity) can make it seem warmer than reported.

If you're like so many people who have moved to Sarasota from all over the world you'll be amazed by our magnificent cloud formations. After chatting with dozens of new residents, I learned that few parts of the world enjoy such an astonishing cloud show.

CLIMATE DATA FOR SARASOTA, FL

January - June

Month	Jan	Feb	Mar	Apr	May	Jun	Year
Record high °F (°C)	89 (32)	88 (31)	90 (32)	94 (34)	95 (35)	100 (38)	100 (38)
Average high °F (°C)	72 (22)	74 (23)	77 (25)	82 (28)	87 (31)	90 (32)	83 (28)
Average low °F (°C)	51 (11)	53 (12)	57 (14)	60 (16)	65 (18)	74 (23)	63 (17)
Record low °F (°C)	23 (−5)	24 (−4)	30 (−1)	38 (3)	46 (8)	52 (11)	20 (−7)
Precipitation inches (mm)	2.94 (74.7)	2.66 (67.6)	3.36 (85.3)	1.85 (47)	2.85 (72.4)	7.41 (188.2)	54.14 (1,375.2)

July - December

Month	Jul	Aug	Sept	Oct	Nov	Dec	Year
Record high °F (°C)	100 (38)	99 (37)	97 (36)	95 (35)	90 (32)	89 (32)	100 (38)
Average high °F (°C)	91 (33)	91 (33)	90 (32)	85 (29)	80 (27)	74 (23)	83 (28)
Average low °F (°C)	73 (23)	73 (23)	72 (22)	65 (18)	59 (15)	53 (12)	63 (17)
Record low °F (°C)	62 (17)	60 (16)	59 (15)	44 (7)	29 (−2)	20 (−7)	20 (−7)
Precipitation inches (mm)	8.71 (221.2)	9.43 (239.5)	7.25 (184.1)	2.88 (73.2)	2.35 (59.7)	2.45 (62.2)	54.14 (1,375.2)

Source: The Weather Channel

Rainy Season

The rainy season runs from June to September. with an average seasonal rainfall of 35 inches. The warmest month during the rainy season is July. The highest recorded temperature in Sarasota was 100 degrees in 1998 and August on average is the wettest month with just under 10 inches.

Our summer rainstorms, usually falling in the afternoon, often include spectacular thunder and lightning displays. But, even during the rainy season, you'll still see plenty of sunshine and twelve hours or more of daylight to enjoy.

Courtesy of: CMS Photography

Dry Season

The dry season spans our winter and spring running from October to May with the lowest humidity levels from December thru February--just in time for good holiday hair. January is the coolest month and November the driest. The lowest recorded temperature was 20 degrees in 1983 and I personally saw snowflakes in 1989.

Mild weather brings the onset of the snowbirds and tourists. The mass arrival of our seasonal residents who come to thaw out and to bask in our warmth and sunshine gives our economy a big bounce. It is also when we locals break out our sweaters, jeans and boots. We're very sensitive to the cooler temperatures. So you'll see us swagger about town in our winter fashions while the snowbirds and tourists shiver in their shorts and tee shirts. Cool winter weather allows us to turn off the AC and to let in cool fresh air. Nothing beats a Florida home with all the sliding glass doors and windows open to welcome gentle breezes. Believe it or not you may need to turn on the central heat or light the fireplace. Be sure to check your fireplace pilot and/or flue for safety. Your first holiday season without snow may be bittersweet, but I promise that a Siesta sandman is just as fun to build as a northern snowman.

47

Sunshine: Enjoy But Be Careful

Appropriately referred to as the Suncoast, we can count on plenty of strong sunlight year-round. Because we are so close to the equator, be cautious and wear sun protective clothing, hats, sunblock and sunglasses. Our reflective water and sand will expose you to the sun while in the water and even under your umbrella. You can still get a golden tan from your day-to-day activities that give you modest exposure to the sun.

Courtesy of: Robert Pope Photography

Hurricane information

The Reality of Living in a Hurricane Area

The year-round warm gentle Gulf waters and refreshing Gulf breezes have an unwelcome cousin--tropical storms and hurricanes. The Atlantic storm season officially begins on June 1st and ends on November 30th each year. Although hurricanes can arrive anytime during that season, September is the most active month. Fortunately, even in an active season, it's extremely rare for a major hurricane to strike the Gulfcoast at or near Sarasota. The last direct hit nearby was in Venice in 1944.

Nonetheless, the potential damage from hurricanes means we must pay close attention to all storms approaching our Atlantic region. Fortunately, modern hurricane forecasting gives us sufficient warning so we have plenty of time to plan and be safe. They also give our local weather anchors some much needed excitement. If you are new to the area, please remember that with a plan are careful preparation, there is no need to panic.

According to the website Hurricane City, Sarasota has experienced a total of 65 storms including both hurricanes and tropical storms throughout the areas recorded history. The October of 1921 Hurricane (storms weren't named in those days), was not a direct hit landing 50 miles to the northwest of Sarasota, but caused damage to the original fish houses that resided along the downtown bayfront. The Suncoast's one and only direct hit occurred in 1944 and blew directly into Venice with 100 mile per hour winds. Thankfully, our area has narrowly missed many storms including Hurricane Charley in 2004, which hit Charlotte County to our south resulting in 60 mile per hour winds in Sarasota. The massive Hurricane Donna in 1960 made landfall further south in Naples, but still produced 90 to 100 mile per hour winds in Sarasota. Even though Sarasota has avoided direct hits for more than a century, we are not invulnerable.

Wind, rain and tornadoes driven by hurricanes and tropical storms affect everyone, not just resident on the coast or on our barrier islands. Therefore, if you live anywhere in Florida, determine your region's evacuation zone. You can find that information on the Sarasota County's Emergency Services website which includes not only your location's hurricane zone but, shelter and hospital information as well.

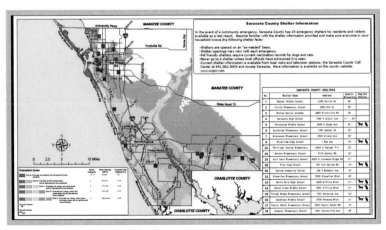

Source: Sarasota County Government www.scgov.net

To prepare for storm season, create a disaster kit that enables you to be self-sufficient for at least one week--that is, without power, water or access to food supplies.

On the Sarasota County's Emergency Services website, you will find a copy of the most current Hurricane Guide with all the information and links for your home, business and pets as well as tips for senior citizens. The Official Hurricane Guide for The Tampa Bay Area which includes Sarasota County is a fantastic handbook for preparing yourself for the storm season. It includes all the information you need for planning and protecting yourself, your home and your loved ones. For the tech savvy there are multiple mobile weather/emergency apps that are available for free download including; Accuweather, Hurricane by American Red Cross, NOAA, The Weather Channel and Weather Underground. Of course, our local weather team alongside the national weather service will keep you informed of the ever changing storm path with constantly updated predictions throughout storm.

As years pass without dangerous or devastating storms, locals tend to become remiss about preparing for storm season. That's not a good idea. When a storm threatens you will hear about hurricane parties and see lots of people attempting to surf the suddenly surfable Gulf waves. Instead, take the intermediate approach. Don't let the local news team terrify you. Perhaps, enjoy a storm party cocktail but please stay out of the rough water. As long as you have a plan in place and are ready for the worst, you will survive the storm season unscathed.

CHAPTER 4

LIVING WELL IN SARASOTA

Cost of Living

Housing

Our region's affordable cost of housing might surprise you. You have certainly seen glossy advertisements for lavish waterfront estates and sprawling golf course mansions. But, Sarasota actually has housing options within everyone's price range. Although the real estate market is experiencing an uptick, current pricing is still well below the 2006-2007 housing boom highs.

Source: Bill Furst Sarasota County Property Appraiser 2014 Annual Report

The median sales price for a single family home in Sarasota County in June 2015 was just $230,000 and the median sales price for condominiums was $210,000. Of course, your choice of neighborhood, housing style, and proximity to the water will impact how much you pay. But, the good news is that you can get to the beach is less than twenty minutes from most Sarasota locations.

When figuring your cost of housing, remember to include homeowner association fees and community assessments within your monthly calculations. Prestigious gated communities and maintenance-free living always bring additional monthly costs. If you don't need those extra luxuries, Sarasota offers a wonderful selection of three bedroom, 2 bath homes with a pool and a two-car garage costing an average price of $375,000. So, living well can easily be within your reach.

Sarasota housing prices compared to desirable areas around the country:

In late 2015, according to the website Zillow, here are the median prices for homes in the following areas:

- San Diego, California $512,000

- Tribeca, New York $3,288,200

- Washington DC, Bloomingdale $688,200

- Seattle, Washington $507,600

- Fairfield, Connecticut $498,400

- Denver, Colorado $449,200

- Coral Gables, Florida $734,100

Utilities
Electricity:

In Sarasota, we pay less for electricity than do other areas around the country and within the state. Although the cost will vary depending on your lifestyle, you won't need to spend a fortune on electricity. Our main electricity provider in the area is Florida Power & Light. They offer complimentary home energy surveys to help residents become more energy efficient. According to the Edison Electric Institute, when comparing the typical 1,000 kWh residential usage in the Winter of 2015 the national average bill was $136.01. FPL came in close to 30% lower than the national average at $99.57. When comparing rates for electric companies across the state of Florida, FPL's annual average for a typical residential monthly bill of 1,000 kWh was $99.57 still below the state average of $118.12.

Natural Gas and Propane:

Yes, Florida uses natural gas as well as propane. In fact, we have a buried propane tank in our backyard that provides fuel for our fireplace and kitchen range. Many communities were developed with access to natural gas and use it to fuel ranges, clothing dryers, water heaters, pool heaters, fireplaces and grills. If gas lines are not available in your area you can purchase or rent a propane tank. If cooking with gas or having access to gas is important to you, have your real estate agent help you to narrow down your home search options. If you are interested in having a generator for backup power supply or to assist with storm fear then having access to natural gas or propane is a real benefit.

Teco Peoples Gas is the main provider of natural gas in our area. But, because you have several options for propane, you should meet with multiple companies to find the best solution for your needs. These companies include: Detweiler's Propane Gas Service, Inc., Flanders Gas, Inc., and Suburban Propane.

Water & Sewer:

We all need it, but there is no quick easy answer for water and sewer service in our region. Your provider truly depends on your location. The regional list below will assist you in connecting with the provider for your area. Please note that some areas, both rural and urban, are still on private septic and well systems.

For irrigation, your property may draw from a well, reclaim water from a lake/pond or metered water meaning from the tap. Be careful if you begin to water the lawn with a metered irrigation system or you will be shocked when your water bill arrives. Lawn watering may also be restricted because of seasonal drought and conservation requirements. So, always check with your area's government website to see what the current restrictions are before watering.

Sarasota County Water Services 941-861-6790

City of Sarasota Public Works 941-955-2325

Town of Longboat Key Public Works 941-316-1988

City of Venice Utilities 941-480-3333

City of North Port Utilities Department 941-240-8000

Because multiple publicly-owned companies provide water and sewer service to the area, the pricing and fee structure varies throughout the county. The 2012 Florida Water Rate Survey conducted by Raftelis Financial Consultants, Inc. is available online with a complete water pricing breakdown. Also, it is good to know that most of the water companies will work with you on a discounted rate if you have a leak, new sod or plantings, or are filling your pool for the first time or need a repair. Be sure to call them first and discuss your project or issue.

Property Taxes

You won't need to fear our property taxes because they are much lower than many states throughout the country.

Comparing Median Property Tax Paid on Homes Across the Nation:

Sarasota, Sarasota County – Florida $2,004

Boston, Suffolk County - Massachusetts $2,936

New York City, Westchester County – New York $8,474

Cleveland, Cuyahoga County - Ohio $2,545

Chicago, Cook County - Illinois $3,494

Fairfield, Essex County – New Jersey $7,801

Arlington County – Virginia $4,498

Sausalito, Marin County – California $5,026

Data from the TaxFoundation.org

All of your tax questions and concerns can be answered by visiting Sarasota County Property Taxes website or calling 941-861-8300.

When comparing Sarasota to other Florida communities here is how we stack up:

Comparing Average Total Millage Rates by City (Millage Rates are Tax Amount per $1000 of Assessed Value):

- Bonita Springs $16

- Cape Coral $21

- Captiva Island $15

- Estero $16

- Ft. Myers Beach $17

- Ft. Myers $22

- Golden Gate Estates $13

- Lehigh Acres $18

- Marco Island $12

- Naples $13

- North Ft. Myers $17

- Port Charlotte $17

- Punta Gorda $17

- *Sarasota $14*

Source: ** Data above from http://www.findsouthwestfloridahomes.com/blog/comparing-sw-florida-county-real-estate-taxes/

Your real estate tax bill in Sarasota County is a combination of ad valorem taxes and non-ad valorem assessments. The tangible tax bill is exclusively an ad valorem tax that is based on the value of the property. Examples include school, county and city taxes. Taxing authorities, listed in the chart below, are responsible for establishing ad valorem millage rates. A millage rate is the rate of tax per thousand of taxable value. Ad valorem taxes are paid in arrears and are based on a true calendar year, January 1 - December 31. To determine your ad valorem tax, multiply the taxable value by the millage rate and divide by 1,000. The example provided by the Sarasota County Property Taxes website is, $100,000 in taxable value with a millage rate of 5.0000 would generate $500 in taxes.

The Sarasota County Property Appraiser is responsible for establishing the value of real property in Sarasota. Market value is established through the appraisal process governed by Florida Law. Market value is set for each property within the county annually on January 1. Don't hunt down the property appraiser just yet; they are not responsible for your tax rates, district budgets, special assessment or the amount of taxes that you pay. The taxable value of your property is calculated by subtracting any exemptions for the assessed value.

Multiple deductions are available for homeowners including The Homestead Exemption of $25,000 for permanent residents, agricultural classified land exemptions, widow/widower exemptions, disability classifications, seniors and veterans exemptions.

Non-ad valorem assessments are based on factors other than the property value such as square footage or number of units. Levying authorities are responsible for setting non-ad valorem assessments amounts and these may or may not be assessed in the calendar year as some are paid in advance. Non-ad valorem assessments include storm water utilities, fire and rescue services and solid waste collections.

In your real estate search you may run across a Community Development District which will also show up in your non-ad valorem tax assessment. A Community Development District or CDD is a local, special purpose government authorized by Chapter 190 of the Florida Statues as an alternative method for managing and financing infrastructure required to support community development. The CDD may impose and levy taxes or assessment or a combination of both on the properties located within its district. Because of the different exemptions available to permanent residents, don't use the current homeowner's tax records as a basis for calculating your property taxes. The current resident may have multiple exemptions for which you may or may not qualify. It may have benefited from the Save our Homes Cap that is placed on the assessed value the year after the property received at Homestead Exemption. This limits the percentage of change in their tax rate.

Therefore you should calculate new taxes based on the amount you paid for the property and the current millage rate. This is also true for estimating homeowners insurance as the current homeowner may have personal property such as jewelry and art work included in their insurance quote or they may have their rates based on inflated boom time value not the current market value of the property.

Services

Safety

The U.S. Department of Justice Uniform Crime Reporting Statistics most recent collection of data indicates that in 2010 Sarasota was ranked 10th place, amongst twenty-six Florida counties of similar population density, for the lowest incidents of violent crimes. We have a variety of departments within the County who provide public safety and service including the all-encompassing Sarasota County Sheriff's Office, Sarasota Police Department assisting the area within the city limits, Town of Longboat Key Police Department, City of Venice Police Department and City of North Port Police Department.

Courtesy of: Sarasota County Sheriff's Office

According to the 2014 Annual Report published by the Sarasota County Sherriff's Office crime in our area dropped nearly 10 percent in 2014 compared to 2013. Major crimes decreased more than 12 percent, violent crime dropped nearly 3 percent and burglary dropped more than 22 percent.

Enjoy the feeling of knowing that you reside in a safe community, but don't overlook the basics: Be alert, lock your homes and cars and use your security alarms because no one is immune to becoming a victim of crime.

Courtesy of: Sarasota County Sheriff's Office

Healthcare
Hospitals

As you might imagine, a community that proudly posts their ER waiting times on billboards throughout the county works extra hard to offer residents and guests quality healthcare and service. Sarasota County has four award winning hospitals to serve residents and visitors that are conveniently located throughout the region.

Courtesy of: Sarasota Memorial Hospital

Sarasota Memorial Hospital is centrally located along Tamiami Trial and spans multiple blocks from Floyd Street to Hillview Street. SMH's sprawling complex is one of the largest public health systems in Florida. Their 819-bed full-service contains a network of outpatient centers, long-term care, rehabilitation and numerous programs with specializations in heart, vascular, cancer and neuroscience services. Sarasota Memorial is also the only hospital currently providing obstetrical services, pediatrics and Level III neonatal intensive care within the County.

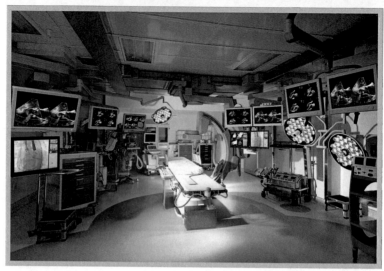

Courtesy of: Sarasota Memorial Hospital

Sarasota Memorial Hospital received the Healthgrades Hospital Award: America's 50 Best™

This Award is America's 50 Best in CMS. It is award code **A50B** 2013, 2012, 2011. America's 50 Best Hospitals are those hospitals that provide the highest quality of care year over year. These hospitals are recognized as the top 1% in the nation for consistent clinical quality based on an analysis of risk-adjusted mortality and complication rates for common procedures and conditions.

Source: Healthgrades.com

Two of our local hospitals are part of Hospital Corporation of America, Doctors Hospital of Sarasota and Englewood Community Hospital. HCA is a Nashville-based national hospital company managing 162 hospitals and 113 surgery centers in 20 states.

Doctors Hospital is located in central Sarasota just north of Bee Ridge Road east of Interstate 75. This 155-bed acute and general care facility provides medical and specialty services as well as outpatient services, diagnostic and rehabilitation services. An intimate hospital set on a beautiful campus Doctors Hospital also offers 24 hour emergency services.

Doctors Hospital received the Healthgrades Hospital Award: Distinguished Hospital Award for Clinical Excellence™

 This Award is Distinguished Hospital Award for Clinical Excellence in CMS. It is award code **DHCE** 2013, 2012. Distinguished Hospitals for Clinical Excellence™ are those hospitals that perform in the top 5% nationally for overall clinical excellence. While many hospitals have specific areas of expertise and high-quality outcomes in those areas, these hospitals exhibit comprehensive high-quality care based on risk-adjusted mortality and complication rates for common procedures and conditions.

Source: Healthgrades.com

Englewood Community Hospital also a member of HCA is located in the southern area of the County located off Pine Street and Medical Boulevard. This boutique 100-bed acute care facility offers a wide variety of healthcare services including general surgery, emergency care, urology and orthopedics.

Englewood Community Hospital received the Healthgrades Hospital Award: General Surgery Excellence Award™

 This Award is General Surgery Excellence Award in CMS. It is award code **GSO** 2012, 2011. The General Surgery Excellence Award recognizes hospitals for superior outcomes in three different areas of general surgery: bowel obstruction, cholecystectomy (gallbladder removal), and gastrointestinal surgeries and procedures. Your risk of complications and death can be significantly lower at these nationally recognized hospitals for general surgery.

Source: Healthgrades.com

Venice Regional Bayfront Health formerlyVenice Regional Medical Center. Centrally located just off South Tamiami Trail on The Rialto and Sovrano Road, this 312-bed regional health care system provides comprehensive health care services across a number of facilities including an acute care hospital, Venice Regional's comprehensive cardiac services, an ambulatory care center and a home health agency. Venice Regional Bayfront Health was recently named by Thomson Reuters one of the Top 50 cardiovascular programs in the country.

Venice Regional Medical Center received the Healthgrades Hospital Award: Patient Safety Excellence Award™

This Award is <u>Patient Safety Excellence Award</u> in CMS. It is award code **PSAFE** 2011. Patient Safety measures how well a hospital prevents infections, medical errors, and other complications based on 14 standard patient safety indicators. On average, patients hospitalized at Patient Safety Excellence Award Hospitals were 52% less likely to experience one of the 14 events compared to lowest-performing hospitals.

Source: <u>Healthgrades.com</u>

Physician's Offices

Our excellent hospital system also makes for a large community of physicians throughout the area. Although choosing a general practitioner or family doctor could be overwhelming, you can simplify your search by utilizing each healthcare provider's search criteria on their website. Most insurance providers' websites will allow you to explore physicians by their age, sex, distance from your location and specializations as well as independent search sites such as <u>Healthgrades</u> and <u>Vitals</u>. Requesting current patient references and reading reviews can also be very helpful in selecting a physician's office that is best suited for your needs. Although we are known as a retirement and tourist area, a growing number of young families are definitely a part of our population. We have an extensive network of pediatricians and child service specialists to fulfill your needs.

Walk-in Clinics

If you are in a hurry, not near the Hospital complexes or without a family physician there are many clinics ready and willing to assist you. According to <u>YellowPages.com</u>, Sarasota County has 351 walk-in clinics or urgent care facilities. This list includes the <u>Sarasota Memorial Hospital Urgent Care</u> centers as well as the new <u>Walgreens Take Care Clinics</u>. So, even if your doctor isn't available, you can avoid the emergency room for basic medical concerns or questions.

Community Blood Center

<u>Suncoast Communities Blood Bank</u> is a not-for-profit, independent blood bank servicing both Sarasota and Manatee counties. They

are graciously supported by individual donors, corporations and foundations. Suncoast Communities Blood Bank's sole purpose is to collect, test, process, match, store and distribute blood products to hospitals and health centers in our region. They make becoming a donor as painless as possible with five locations spread throughout the county as well as the traveling Blood Mobile. Blood Bank hours, directions, Blood Drive locations and the Blood Mobile schedule can be found online or by calling 1-866-97-BLOOD.

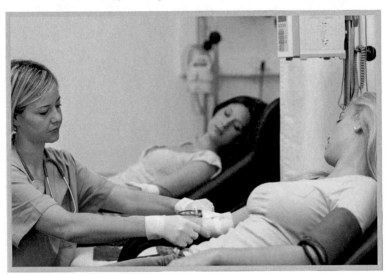

Veterans Service
Sarasota Veterans Center

U.S. Department of Veterans Affairs has a Vet Center in Sarasota ready to assist all veterans with their needs and guide them in the right direction. They are located at 4801 Swift Road - Suite A, Sarasota, FL. 34231 and their phone number is 941-927-8285.

Sarasota Community-Based Outpatient Clinic

The VA primary care facility assists veterans with primary care, mental health care, audiology, EKG services, phlebotomy, social work and pharmacist consultation. Referrals for specialty care are also addressed at this facility. Specialty care and extensive surgery are handled approximately an hour drive north at the Bay Pines VA Medical Center. The Sarasota Community-Based Outpatient Clinic is located at 5682 Bee Ridge Road - Suite 100, Sarasota, FL. 34233 and their phone number is 941-371-3349. The Bay Pines VA Healthcare System's main facility is located at 10000 Bay Pines Blvd, Bay Pines, FL. 33744 and their phone number is 727-398-6661.

Sarasota National Cemetery

With the passage of the National Cemetery Expansion Act of 2003, Sarasota had the privileged of being chosen as a national burial site. The U.S. Department of Veterans Affairs selected Sarasota after a nationwide demographic study identifying our area as having a dense veteran population with a lack of burial options. In 2007 the J. Arlin Hawkins family-owned and operated ranch site was purchased by the government for the creation of the 295-acre national cemetery. This pastoral site is located along Clark Road (State Road 72) approximately four miles east of Interstate 75. Formally dedicated in 2008 the cemetery will serve veterans' needs for the next fifty years. The Sarasota National Cemetery is proud to be the sixth national cemetery in the state of Florida.

Hospice
Tidewell Hospice

"Helping people live well by providing care, comfort and compassion" is the mission of Tidewell Hospice, Sarasota largest not-for-profit hospice network serving more than 1,200 patients daily in Sarasota, Manatee, Charlotte and DeSoto counties. Founded in 1980, Tidewell assists patients with any illness who are facing a predictable prognosis of six months or less. Their program provides care and support to anyone in need regardless of their ability to pay. Tidewell assists patients wherever their services are required including within a private residence, hospital, assisted-living facility, nursing home or any of its seven hospice houses. For more information on Tidewell Hospice visit their website or call toll free number at 855-tidewell.

CHAPTER 5

CHOOSING WHERE TO LIVE

A Variety of Housing Choices

From lavish beachfront mansions to rustic cabins along the Myakka River, your housing options in Sarasota are endless. Accommodating every lifestyle, Sarasota's choices include:

- Condominiums available in high- rise, midrise and even low-rise buildings

- Villas both paired(attached) and detached

- Townhomes and carriage homes

- Single family homes in every imaginable size

- Manufactured homes, yes these are still available in our area

When selecting your residence of choice, consider your lifestyle preference, whether you will be a fulltime or part-time resident and your age/health. Whatever you're looking for, you can find it in our Sarasota community:

- Dozens of maintenance-free communities are available if you don't want to handle your own exterior upkeep personally. This option is especially popular for seasonal residents.

- If you need extra help because of age or health concerns, we have a large selection of assisted and senior living facilities offering residents a full range of medical assistance as well as senior social activities.

- Are you a sports enthusiast? If so, you'll find lots of golf course, country club, boating and equestrian lifestyle options.

- You can choose to be part of a large or small neighborhood, a gated community or being a member of a country club.

- Golf fanatics and casual golfers will find plenty of home choices, many with mesmerizing views.

- Boaters or sunset lovers can choose from waterfront homes on either canal, bay, Intracoastal or Gulf front homes.

- If you value walkability, living downtown, near Southside Village or even Siesta Key will meet your needs.

- Whether you want to be close to your neighbors or insulated on country acreage, you have plenty to choose from.

Courtesy of: CMS Photography

Courtesy of: Robert Pope Photography

Courtesy of: Robert Pope Photography

Luckily, you can narrow the infinite home choices into a perfect fit by using the geographic and community information we provide in Chapter 2 and just below. You can then conduct internet searches to match your lifestyle. And then, find a professional Realtor to complete the search.

Consider your lifestyle checklist a priority over your housing option as you may be surprised by the size and attention to detail available in some of our townhomes and villas. Also, searching by price alone will have you running all over the county. Determine your price range and preferred lifestyle first to see what is available. Then continue your search from there. If you're a boater, you don't need to look at homes near Myakka Park. And, if acreage and horses are critical to you, don't spend time looking on Siesta Key.

On the other hand, many of our popular neighborhoods will offer a collection of different housing choices within the community affording a little something for everyone. For example, The Oaks has a very prestigious golf course and exclusive country club. But, the community includes a mix of large waterfront homes, condominiums, golf course frontage homes and smaller maintenance-free villas.

Even if you find the perfect house in a community that lacks some vital lifestyle activities, there is generally an easy solution. Most of the county clubs in the area offer social memberships for non-residents just as there are marinas available for boat storage for non-waterfront residents and boarding sites for horse owners.

The Online Real Estate Search Process

Sarasota County is an expansive community with many neighborhoods and a wide selection of housing options available. Whether you are renting or buying, over 90 percent of all real estate searches begins online.

Rental Searches

Because we are both a seasonal location and a tourist destination, your rental search will uncover a wide range of pricing depending on time of year and duration. Many rentals are only for the "season" without annual availability, so search and inquire carefully. Rental search sites for apartments include the Apartment Guide and ForRent.com. If you are looking for single family homes or condominiums, websites such as Jennette Properties, Siesta 4-Rent specializing on Siesta key, and Rossi & Company Inc can be of great assistance. The local newspaper Sarasota Herald Tribune as well as Craigslist can also be great resources for searching your rental needs.

Home Buying Searches

Buyers have many good online choices for residential real estate searches. In Sarasota County, Realtors list their properties for sale in the Multiple Listing Service (MLS), which feeds to all the secondary sites like Realtor.com, Zillow, Homes.com and many more.

Individual real estate firms and agents also host websites that allow you to search for homes although these sites may be structured to showcase their own firm's or agents' listings. Once you've fine-tuned your home buying options via online search, you will almost certainly want to work with a professional Realtor.

If you elect to become a part-time resident of our beautiful city, multiple companies in the area provide "home caretaking" services. Sarasota Home Watch, Key Concierge, Always Home, and American Home Watch are a sampling of the available companies in the area. These concierge service firms give homeowners peace of mind while being away. Their services can be customized, but typically include: watching over the residence, inspecting for water leaks and security breaches, verification of lawn and pool services being performed, checking for running faucets and flushing toilets, securing a home before a storm, inspecting the property for pests and even watering of plants.

State of the Real Estate Market:

By the end of 2012 the west coast of Florida gratefully began to see the light at the end of the Great Recession's long, dark tunnel. Buyer confidence has begun to accelerate. And, housing inventories are decreasing. A seller's market may well be on the way. Both buyers and sellers are accepting the new norms of a more conservative real estate market. Sellers are now getting fair value for their properties. Buyers are finding that the stories of deals and steals have past them by.

Our renewed, post-recession population growth is a critical factor both in our region's economy and in the real estate market. The Suncoast economy is recovering at an unexpectedly brisk pace. During 2012 the area's population growth rate more than tripled from the previous year. Sarasota County experienced a 1.2 percent population increase for the 2012 year.

Since 2012 the Sarasota area's real estate market has been steadily improving, with record sales and shrinking inventory. We are seeing new developments popping up throughout the many regions of the community with new construction on the continual rise and new product suppling buyers with options during times of limited inventory.

2014 real estate results demonstrated an all-time record of 11,550 closed transactions, surpassing the 2004 total of 11,482. "This is truly historic news, and clearly demonstrates our region is experiencing a remarkable success story in real estate," said Associated President Stafford Starcher in the Realtor Association of Sarasota and Manatee January 23, 2015 press release.

We also continue to see a dramatic reduction in distressed property sales with a reduced quantity of short sales and foreclosures. Distressed property sales have dropped from 51 percent in Q4 2010 to just 20% percent of the overall sales in December 2014.

Monthly Market Summary— June 2015
Single Family Homes in Sarasota County

	June 2015	June 2014	Percent Change Year-over-Year
Closed Sales	831	727	14.3%
Cash Sales	385	391	-1.5%
New Pending Sales	657	627	4.8%
New Listings	778	772	0.8%
Median Sale Price	$230,000	$195,000	17.9%
Average Sale Price	$326,134	$310,929	4.9%
Median Days on Market	45	66	-31.8%
Avg. Percent of Original List Price Received	94.5%	91.9%	2.8%
Pending Inventory	1076	1079	-0.3%
Inventory (Active Listings)	2366	2927	-19.2%
Months Supply of Inventory	3.5	4.6	-25.3%

Source: SREALTOR® Association of Sarasota and Manatee

Renting vs. Buying on the Suncoast

If you are brand new to the area, you may want to rent while deciding upon your ideal home purchase type and location. But, buying a home may cost you less in the end. "Buying a home is more affordable than renting now in almost every part of the United States," said Jed Kolko, chief economist for Trulia. According to Money.cnn.com the average rent in Sarasota has jumped 12.9 percent year-over-year, the biggest increase of any of the 100 largest metro areas Trulia surveyed.

Whether you buy or rent, the cost of moving, decorating and general utilities remain the same. Purchasing a property requires additional closing costs and taxes for buyers versus the deposits necessary for those who rent. Mortgage interest and real estate tax deductions are an appealing tax benefit for homeowners, while some rentals may include lawn care and a few utilities.

Because mortgage interest rates remain exceptionally low compared to historical norms, home ownership often costs less per month than renting. There are some excellent websites with online calculators to assist in comparing the costs of renting vs. buying a home. Try the Smart Money Magazine website www.smartmoney.com/personal-finance/real-estate/to-rent-or-to-buy-9687 or the Freddie Mac online calculator at www.freddiemac.com/corporate/buyown/english/calcs_tools/ to assist in making your decision.

As we hopefully learned from the last real estate boom and bust, think of your house or condo as a home to love rather than as a surefire investment.

Real Estate Services

The real estate business is a large sector of our local economy, according Realtor.com there are 4273 agents in Sarasota County and 577 real estate firms. A great place to start your search for a real estate profession is the REALTOR® Association of Sarasota and Manatee.

Of course, just walking through Sarasota you'll surely meet lots of friendly realtors. As local ambassadors for our magnificent town, realtors provide a wealth of information about how to enjoy life in Sarasota.

Every recognizable national real estate company brand is represented here as well as some very strong local firms. In the end, you need to feel comfortable with the company and the professional you choose.

Once you have found the perfect home you will have many options for "closing" your transaction. Local Sarasota buyers commonly use either title companies or real estate attorneys.

Shopping

Grocery and Gourmet Items

We have a plethora of food markets that stock the ingredients for creating any tasty delight you desire. Sarasota is home to multiple fresh markets, specialty grocery stores, farmers markets, popular natural food retailers, large grocery chains and bulk box suppliers.

Courtesy of: CMS Photography

You'll find the big grocery chain stores, Publix, Winn-Dixie and Walmart Neighborhood Market conveniently located throughout the county. These large supermarkets provide much more than standard grocery fare, typically including onsite pharmacies, liquor stores, full-service deli departments, butcher ships, bakeries, floral sections and even fresh sushi.

Both Wal-Mart and Target have introduced grocery departments and now compete with the major chains. There are two Wal-Mart Supercenters one located in Osprey/Nokomis and one in Venice featuring complete grocery stores, in addition to standard Wal-Mart located on Cattleman Road. The Super Target on University Parkway also has a full grocery department. Balancing out your grocery needs there is a new Costco Wholesale located in Palmer Ranch and a Sam's

Club at the intersection of Cattleman Road and Fruitville Road near Interstate 75, both of these bulk retailers require membership but offer great savings.

Two farm stand produce markets are open daily in Sarasota, Detwiler's Farm Market , Fruitville Grove. Jessica's Organic Farm is open only on weekends. They provide an abundant supply of the season's freshest produce. Within the Amish Village located along Bahia Vista Street, you will also find Yoder's Produce Market and other smaller Amish and Mennonite harvest stands. Be sure to check out their hand crafted cheeses, local honey, baked goods and other scrumptious treats.

Courtesy of: Ed Wisburn Photography

Attending all of the local farmers markets throughout the county could become a full-time hobby. The Sarasota Farmers Market, a local tradition since 1979, is open every Saturday from 7am to 12pm rain or shine. It lures hundreds of Sarasotans onto the downtown streets for a fun morning's shopping. Radiating from the intersection of Lemon Avenue and Main Street, over 70 vendors set up shop selling fresh flowers, produce, fish, pasta, nuts, oils, soaps, furniture and everything in between. From October through April, the new Phillippi Farmhouse Market is rapidly growing popular with over 40 vendors. Open Wednesdays from 9am to 2pm it's located in central

Sarasota at the Phillippi Estate Park located just off Tamiami Trail south of Proctor Road

The Venice Farmer's Market also takes place every Saturday morning from 8am to 12pm on Tampa Avenue between Nokomis and Nausau Avenues. Also on Saturday mornings at the corner of Proctor Road and Beneva Road from 8am to 1pm is the Central Sarasota Farmers Market. Last but not least, the Siesta Key Farmers Market takes place at Davidson's Plaza on Ocean Boulevard on Sundays from 8am to 2pm.

Specialty local grocery stores and gourmet shops are a staple throughout the region. Siesta Key has no chain supermarkets and is home to the Crescent Beach Grocery and the original Siesta Market, which has recently been sold to and we are waiting for the renewed market to open soon. An excellent mainland choice is Morton's Gourmet Market in Southside Village. These specialty stores provide exceptional customer service and top quality merchandise. Fish markets, butcher shops and gourmet food retailers are also plentiful throughout the area. Whatever your global heritage, Sarasota likely has a specialty store stocking the food treasures of your homeland.

Courtesy of: CMS Photography

Among our many sources for natural and organic food supplies a Whole Foods downtown, two Earth Origins markets, multiple Richards Foodporiums, and a new Trader Joes.

Wine and Spirits

Wine, beer and liquor can be purchased at all of the local grocery stores as well as specialty retailers. Among the dozens of liquor stores throughout the County are <u>Norman's Liquors</u>, <u>Sarasota Liquor Locker</u>, many <u>ABC Fine Wine & Spirits</u> locations and <u>Sarasota Fine Wine</u> to name just a few. There is also a brand new <u>Total Wine</u> on the South Trail just south of Beneva Road. Wine vendors and tastings are popular throughout the area <u>Michael's Wine Cellar</u> has a full calendar of tastings and events for the wine enthusiasts. For craft beer connoisseurs, try <u>Mr. Beery's</u> located in Gulf Gate whose array of luscious libations will quench your thirst.

Courtesy of: Michael's on East

All-Inclusive shopping centers

Strip style malls are conveniently spread throughout the county, normally anchored by a major grocery chain, Target or Wal-Mart with lots of stores, restaurants and service establishments.

We have three enclosed shopping malls: <u>Westfield Southgate</u> in central Sarasota at Tamiami Trail and Bee Ridge Road, and the <u>Westfield Sarasota Square</u> at the intersection of Tamiami Trail and Beneva Road. and the brand new Mall at <u>University Town Center</u> located at the intersection of University Parkway and Cattlemen Road. The Southgate location is anchored by a Macy's and a Cobb Cinebistro currently under construction with plans to open in early 2016. The Sarasota Square location is home to the new Costco, an AMC theatre, Macy's, Sears and JCPenneys.

Opening in October of 2015, The Mall at University Town Center (UTC) is home to Saks Fifth Avenue, Macy's, Dillard's and over 100 stores and restaurants. This 880,000 square-foot, two-story retail mecca is the first mall to be built of its size in the nation since the Great Recession.

Shopping Areas

<u>St. Armand's Circle</u> is the premier shopping destination on the Suncoast. This open air shopping district includes boutiques, art galleries, restaurants and a wide array of services.

Located between the businesses, restaurants and services of Downtown Sarasota and the Island of Venice, plenty of fun and unique shopping areas feature trendy boutiques, national retail brands, and a variety of art galleries.

Southside Village located in the West of the Trail area is home to many hip local restaurants, services, Morton's Gourmet Market and a nice collection of locally owned and operated retail establishments.

Scattered among the souvenir shops, beach bars and festive seafood cafés, Siesta Key Village is home to swimwear, beach-themed stores, and the upscale Foxy Lady clothing boutique.

A quick day trip to Arcadia can satisfy your antiquing urges. Arcadia is a memorable small town on our eastern border in DeSoto County. This picturesque town offers shopping adventures with treasure-filled antique stores lining the streets. The <u>Antique Association of Arcadia</u> coordinates antique fairs that run monthly April thru December.

Flea Markets

Yes, we still have flea markets. To beat the heat they are partially or fully air conditioned.

The Red Barn Flea Market on 1st Street in Bradenton is a 145,000 square foot former lumber yard. It's been converted into a traditional flea market with plaza shops, a food court, and open-air farmers markets. Two-thirds of the facility is air conditioned for year round shopping comfort. The Red Barn Flea Market is open Tuesday thru Sunday. Their hours of operation vary seasonally, so check their website at redbarnfleamarket.com or call 941-747-3794 before planning your shopping excursion.

The Dome Flea Market and Farmers Market in Venice just off State Road 776 is open on Friday, Saturday and Sunday throughout the year. Open since 1974, this legendary market appropriately sits under a large, air-conditioned dome. The Dome is home to over 300 vendor booths.

Furniture & Design

As new residents and new homes spark our local economy, it's only natural that furniture and design companies are also plentiful and prosperous. To create your own "Florida Look", you can count on plenty of guidance from savvy local retailers and interior designers.

If you don't consider interior design an enjoyable hobby, you can give the work to one of our talented designers. And, if you're buying new, many buyers are now choosing fully furnished homes with assistance from the builder. That's a big reason furnished model homes in our area sell so quickly.

When deciding the décor for your new home our local furniture and design stores are a great resource. Most major furniture retailers have stores here in addition to a great selection of local shops. On the local scene check out the fantastic finds at Bacon's, Baer's, Kalins, Pomaro Shop, Sarasota Collection Home Store, Living Walls, Home Resource, Robb & Stucky and The Furniture Warehouse. There is a store to suit everyone's taste and design style. A great local establishment the

Pamero Shop specializes in "The Florida Look" with an exciting, constantly changing selection of accessories, furniture, lighting, rugs and so much more. Also available are the national names you know including; American Signature Furniture, Ethan Allen, Havertys, Rooms to Go, Lazy Boy, Pier 1 Imports, Crate & Barrel and Pottery Barn… the list is endless. There is also an IKEA just an hour away in Tampa.

Home Accessories & Much More

The wonderful Home Goods is located on Bee Ridge Road. And, there is a substantial T.J. Maxx & More in Venice. All the shopping districts have art galleries, linen stores and accessory boutiques. The Bed Bath & Beyond, Marshalls, Ross and Stein Mart are located on University Parkway, in the Gulf Gate area and in Venice (except Bed Bath & Beyond).

Resale shops like Designing Women's Boutique and the Women's Exchange receive a fresh supply of gently used items daily and are worth regular visits. The Habitat Restore and Goodwill also have fabulous finds as they offer free pick up and estate removal. Sarasota Architectural Salvage and Sarasota Trading Company are a treasure trove of unique and eclectic finds both old and new.

Courtesy of: CMS Photography

Dressing for the Florida Lifestyle

To assist in acquiring your new Suncoast fashion style, here are some tips from the local experts, Lorry Eible & Lori Ann Steiner, owners of Foxy Lady who have been dressing Sarasotans for over 40 years. *"Light weight natural fabrics are your best bet for staying cool, while layering in the winter months assists with being adaptable as the temperature rises throughout the day. Ladies can enjoy open toe, strappy shoes as well as sandals most of the year, although we do enjoy breaking out the boots at the first sign of cooler weather, which sometimes means temperatures in the low 70's. White can be worn all year as well black, which tends to be northeastern fashion stable, both can also work here on the Suncoast, the inventive use of accessories, shoes and handbags allows for multi-seasoning your white and black wears.*

Courtesy of: Lorry Eible & Lori Ann Steiner of the Foxy Lady

Sophisticated comfortable style sums up the Suncoast fashion scene; whether you enjoy wearing bright beachy prints or neutrals you will find that almost anything goes. Our melting pot of city has created a wonderful fashion fusion, you will rarely see anyone dressed the same and we would not have it any other way."

Locating clothing, shoe and accessory retailers that fit your new Suncoast style will take just a few trips to the local shopping districts to search out the stores that suit your new more casual fashion flair. Sarasota is full of trendy boutiques, fantastic resale shops and national retailers. So, shop your way to uncovering a fresh, cool new look.

Just a reminder: Think cool, comfortable, beachy sophisticated. Most restaurants happily accommodate men wearing nice shorts and a golf shirt and ladies flaunting fashionable sundresses.

Courtesy of: Lorry Eible & Lori Ann Steiner of the Foxy Lady

CHAPTER 6
NEVER A SHORTAGE OF THINGS TO DO

Arts, Culture & Music

The Sarasota Suncoast offers one of Florida's most vibrant cultural and arts scenes. We offer an artistic array of highly acclaimed professional theater groups, <u>Florida State University Center for the Performing Arts</u> complex, an <u>opera house</u>, <u>ballet</u> companies, the <u>Van Wezel Preforming Arts Center</u>, the <u>Ringling Museum of Art</u>, The <u>Ringling College of Art and Design</u> and a host of over thirty local art galleries. Our cultural and art activities provide year round entertainment options for Sarasota residents and visitors.

Van Wezel Performing Arts Center

The <u>Van Wezel Performing Arts Center</u> performance calendar is replete with an extraordinary range of artists and acts from superstar performers like Diana Ross, John Legend, Queen Latifah, John Lithgow and Sheryl Crow to Broadway acts such as "Mamma Mia," "Les Miserables," "Catch Me If You Can," "The Addams Family" and "Rock of Ages". You'll also love classical performances from visiting symphony orchestras. Known by locals as "The Purple Cow", an endearing pseudonym for this unforgettably colorful bayfront building, the Van Wezel's controversial design was conceived by William Wesley Peters of Taliesin Associated Architects of the Frank Lloyd Wright Foundation. His inspiration came from two seashells from the Sea of Japan, which are still on display within the Hall.

The legendary purple color scheme was selected by Olgivanna Lloyd Wright, Wright's widow, resulting in the colorful nickname.

Ringling Museum

You'll need at least a weekend to enjoy all that The Ringling has to offer. Recently acquired by Florida State University, the marvelous Ringling Museum of Art includes the Museum, the Ringling residence known as the Ca' d'Zan, a Circus Museum, Mable's rose garden, a Secret Garden, and two onsite restaurants--The Banyan Café and Treviso.

The Museum of Art houses wonderful works by Old Masters of painting and sculpture including Rubens, van Dyck, Velazquez, Titian, Tintoretto, Verones, El Greco, and many more. The Museum mounts special exhibitions throughout the year which showcase diverse collections of art from around the world.

The Ca d'Zan is a stunning display of Venetian Gothic architecture. Constructed in 1924–1925 this magnificent 36,000 square foot residence underwent a comprehensive restoration that began in 2002. The six year, $15 million project restored the Ca' d'Zan to the glory of the Ringling family's era.

Courtesy of: The John and Mable Ringling Museum of Art, the State Art Museum of Florida

Courtesy of: Detlev von Kessel - pix360

Sarasota Opera

The Sarasota Opera offers an inspirational calendar of performances including "Il trovatore," "The Barber of Seville," "The Flying Dutchman," "Jerusalem" and "Die Fledermaus," as well as educational and youth outreach programs. Located in downtown Sarasota, the historic opera house completed a $20 million dollar renovation in 2008 restoring the 1926 theatre to its original brilliance. Opera News, New York says about the experience of attending a performance, " *With the dimensions of the Opera House, which most almost guarantee an engaging experience between the audience and singers, and DeRenzi's full throttle approach to each work, whether he's conducting it or not, a dull performance at the Sarasota Opera is hard to come by.*"

Sarasota Ballet

Critically acclaimed by the New York and European press the Sarasota Ballet is the only professional ballet company on the Florida Gulf Coast. The Sarasota Ballet School employs current or former professional dancers to provide professional ballet instruction to students of all ages. Presenting full-length classical ballets and world premieres, the Sarasota Ballet offers a unique and wide-ranging repertoire of performances that have never been seen in Florida and rarely in America.

**Ricardo Rhodes and Christine Peixoto in
Ricardo Graziano's Symphony of Sorrows
Photo Courtesy of: The Sarasota Ballet, Photographer:
Frank Atura**

Sarasota Orchestra

The Sarasota Orchestra performs more than a hundred classical, pop and family concerts each year. Originally The Florida West Coast Symphony, the 80-member Sarasota Orchestra has been entertaining local audiences for over 60 years.

The Youth Orchestra Program works with students from the third grade through high school in symphonic music. By expanding students' skills in a fun learning environment, the nationally acclaimed artistic staff, conductors and coaches have created an exemplary youth program.

Even More Cultural Riches During the Year

The few examples above are just a sampling of the cultural, art and music activities available on the Suncoast. Multiple art shows, gallery walks and performance events include: The Chalk Festival, Crystal Classic Sand Master Sculpturing Competition, Sarasota Film Festival, and Sarasota Blues Fest. Gastronomic Delights

Courtesy of: CMS Photography

Sarasota is an epicurean's haven with over a thousand restaurants for all your culinary cravings. Sarasota boasts a thriving dining scene from Zagat-rated elegant fine dining to shore side flip-flop fish shack fare.

In addition, tasty adventures are always within your reach as the region is home to the:

- Forks and Corks Wine & Food Festival in January

- Taste of the Suncoast in March

- Florida Winefest & Auction in April

- Savor Sarasota Restaurant Week in June

Our notorious annual firefighters food challenges take place throughout the year, including rib and chili cook-offs. The funds raised support the Sarasota Fire Fighter's Benevolent Fund. If you want to learn while dining, many local eateries offer themed dining experiences/pairings with expert chefs and sommeliers as well as culinary classes.

We have wonderful print and online guides to help you experience all that Sarasota has to offer

- Sarasota Magazine Dining Guide is a great start on your epicurean adventure.

- Edible Sarasota is a local magazine covering the Suncoast food scene

- The Three Kitcheneers is a witty blog featuring recipes and articles.

- The Sarasota-Manatee Originals website features a group of locally owned and operated restaurants that have teamed up to promote and support independent restaurants serving fresh, local flavor.

Dining on the Suncoast

To help you narrow your bountiful dining choices, Jeff and I decided to share some favorite local spots.

To grab a quick, healthy lunch, Simon's Coffee House on Tamiami Trail is outstanding. We also enjoy The Corkscrew Deli in the Landings, whose creative selection of Boars Head sandwiches are tasty and filling. Because I work downtown, I have an abundance of choices. When watching my waist line, I grab a salad from Duval's New World Café or First Watch. For a more robust meal,

I indulge in the quattro formaggi at Café Americano or a juicy burger from Patrick's 1481.

We have loads of dinner choices, too. If we want to enjoy down home cooking, we head out to J.R.'s Old Packinghouse for fried catfish or country fried steak. Their bluegrass music and rustic atmosphere are a nice change after a formal workday. Libby's Cafe & Bar in the Southside Village has a great bar scene with a large menu of both food and wine. For informal indoor or outdoor waterfront dining we enjoy the Table Creekside on Phillippi Creek. Their roman caesar salad is out of this world and their cheesecake dessert is to die for.

If we are feeling fancy, Miguel's, a family-owned French restaurant on Siesta Key offers excellent tableside preparation of their Caesar salad and Dover sole. We also love Roy's where the Asian fusion cuisine and personal service never disappoint. Our prime pick for a romantic evening is Michael's on East where amorous piano music sets the mood. They have sensational steaks but we love their white truffle macaroni and cheese.

Courtesy of: Michael's on East

Marina Jack offers unique land and sea dining adventures. The Marina Jack II dinner boat sets sail on relaxing dinner cruises. If you'd rather stay on dry land, then try their casual portside open-air cafe with live music or the elegant second floor dining room with panoramic vistas. Sarasota is truly the place to indulge you inner foodie. Enjoy.

Jeff & Tracy Eisnaugle, local Sarasota Foodies

Night Life

It's not all about cultural and culinary activities in Sarasota. We also have plenty of hot spots for a night out on the town. The Gulf Gate district, Southside Village, Downtown areas, St. Armand's Circle and Siesta Village provide great localized zones with a high concentration of restaurants, pubs, taverns and night spots allowing patrons to safely walk from establishment to establishment for a fun night out. No matter where you wet your whistle you'll find bar mates and dance partners of every age from all over the world.

The Music Scene

Our eclectic music scene satisfies every taste from acoustic blues, to tropical steel drums, oldies, rock and roll, and Latin salsa. Whatever music you fancy, you can dig it on the Suncoast. Now, we've even gone Country in central Sarasota with the new White Buffalo Saloon which features country music, live performances, line dancing and a full menu. Ivory Lounge on Main Street hosts a wide range of events for the twenty-something crowd as well as Karaoke every Tuesday night. The Gator Club also located downtown, the Five O'clock Club in the Southside Village and the Beach Club on Siesta Key showcase talented local bands including The Boneshakers, Democracy, Kettle of Fish, Kara Nally Band and the Nick Levalley Band. A hidden local treasure,

J.R's Old Packinghouse Café, is tucked along the eastern side of town near Cattleman Road and Palmer Boulevard. This longstanding celery packing warehouse is home to live acoustic folk, blues and bluegrass music Monday thru Saturday. There is nothing fancy about J.R's just ice cold beer, great food and memorable entertainment.

Summer Nights All Year Long

While there are numerous reasons to fall in love with Sarasota and it's surrounding area, one of my favorites is the weather, particularly at night.

Sure we love our hot days at the beach, out on the water or teeing up on the course, however it's not until the sun goes down that Sarasota really comes alive.

I particularly enjoy sitting outside at one of the wonderful Downtown Sarasota restaurants on Main Street, enjoying a cool drink with friends, all while soaking in the sights and sounds of a summer night out on the town.

With nighttime weather staying mild year round, enjoying outdoor dining and entertainment is easy. Whether it's enjoying a fresh Gimlet at the open air Shore on St. Armand's Circle, or people

Courtesy of: Daniel Volz

watching with one of the infused Mojito creations at Clasico on Main Street, Cucumber Martinis at Selva, Ultra-Premium Tequila at Tequila Cantina, or an old fashioned Rusty Nail at State Street Eating House, there's something for everyone's taste here.

Here in Sarasota we truly enjoy the best of both worlds: the sophisticated style of living in Southwest Florida's premier cultural destination, and the laid back casual Gulf Coast attitude.

Just be warned, if you visit, you may end up moving here. I did!

Daniel Volz - Adventurer, Epicurean and Resident of Sarasota for over 15 years

Sports & Fitness

When you think of Suncoast sports, don't imagine shuffleboard or water aerobics. We are much more active than that.

Because we are an energetic community with miles of bike lanes and sidewalks, you are never alone on the roadways. For runners and cyclists, you have many groups to join as well as many races, fun runs and triathlons each year. Don't overlook swimming. With miles of Gulf Coast shoreline, you won't have to wait for a lane at the pool.

If you are interested in group sports, you'll find everything imaginable in Sarasota: Softball, rowing, rugby, golf, boxing, martial arts, Frisbee golf, and CrossFit training. If you can think of a sports or fitness activity, someone here is organizing it.

Golf

John Hamilton Gillespie is believed to have constructed the first golf course in the country right here in Sarasota. So, our love of the game of golf goes way back. With public and private courses dispersed throughout the region, you have limitless options for picking up a game. Designers like Arnold Palmer, Jack Nicklaus and Robert Trent Jones Jr. have created courses that are both scenic and challenging. Reciprocal privileges and discounted summer rates expand your course choices. **Tip:** To check out a wide selection of courses is to pick up a Big Summer Golf Card, which provides discounts and access to area courses during the slower yet hotter summer months.

Not yet a golfer? Lessons are a great way to learn the sport and to meet other newbies to the links. Check out your local golf shop or ACE (Adult & Community Enrichment) calendar for options.

Courtesy of: CMS Photography

Tennis

If you're a tennis enthusiast, you're also in luck. Tennis is very popular in Sarasota with multiple clubs and locally-hosted tournaments. Close by in Bradenton, Nick Bollettieri founded the renowned IMG Sports

Academy for tennis instruction. World tennis greats have trained at IMG including Andre Agassi, Boris Becker, Jim Courier, Monica Seles, Maria Sharapova and The Williams sisters. But, even amateurs can get top training at the IMG Academy.

Whatever your skill level, you can work on your game at multiple facilities in the region including Bath & Racquet Fitness Club, Serendipity Racquet Club, The Meadows Country Club, The Oaks Club, The Longboat Key Club as well as public courts placed throughout the county including Siesta Public Beach and Longboat Key Public Tennis Center. Tennis courts and lessons are easy to find, so give it a swing.

Courtesy of: CMS Photography

Parks & Gardens

One of our 14 reasons for moving to Sarasota is our vast array of nature parks and nationally recognized beaches. Our parks abound with athletics, recreation, community center activities, rowing, and water sports. We have repurposed land and dedicated it to wildlife preservation and to our residents' enjoyment. County park facilities are also available for private functions and events. Contact Sarasota County Parks & Recreation for additional information.

Two of the largest parks in the area are Myakka State Park and Oscar Scherer State Park.

Myakka State Park

Courtesy of: Florida Department of Environmental Protection

Myakka State Park was originally part of Bertha Palmer's ranchland which she bequeathed to the county for preservation and recreational use. Located in the eastern part of the county Myakka State Park is one of the oldest and largest state parks with 57 square miles of woodlands, prairies and wetlands along the Myakka River. The park offers camping, hiking, air boat tours, bike rentals, birding, canoe and kayak rentals, fishing, picnic areas, concessions, guided safari trams, horse trails and a canopy walk. You'll love the undisturbed wildlife and foliage at Myakka State park.

Oscar Scherer State Park

Oscar Scherer State Park is located along the Tamiami Trail in Osprey, a beautiful section of land surrounding the South Creek, a blackwater stream that flows into the Gulf of Mexico. In 1955, Elsa Scherer Burrows bequeathed 462 acres of land to the state of Florida for use as a park, in memory of her inventor father, Oscar Scherer.

After a year of preparation, Oscar Scherer State Recreation Area was opened to the public in 1956. In 1991, an additional 922 acres were purchased as part of the P2000 initiative. This increased the park's total acreage to 1384 acres.

The South Creek offers wonderful canoeing and kayak adventures, as well as swimming in Lake Osprey. Fifteen miles of trails make for perfect hiking, bicycling and observing the native wildlife. The park offers dedicated camping, hiking, biking, birding, canoeing, kayaking, fishing and picnic areas. The onsite nature center with exhibits and videos about the park is open for visitors. Popular youth group programs also utilize the campsites.

Marie Selby Botanical Gardens

Marie Selby Botanical Gardens was an incredible gift to the community upon Marie Selby's death in 1971. "For the enjoyment of the general public" was the wish of Mrs. Selby. This Mother Nature spectacular rests on 14 acres adjacent to Sarasota Bay. It includes the original Selby home as well as an adjoining property that currently serves as the Gardens' Museum. The Botanical Gardens maintain a plant collection of more than 20,000 greenhouse plants plus thousands more species in the surrounding outdoor gardens. The eight greenhouses onsite contain unusual flora that support their botany department's research and education. They are the headquarters for the Bromeliad, Gesneriad, and Orchid Research Centers, and the Selby Gardens' Herbarium and Molecular Laboratory. Selby Gardens attracts more than 180,000 visitors each year with lectures, exhibits, garden tours, programs and camps. The soon-to-be completed Children's Rainforest Garden will be an extraordinary interactive experience.

Sarasota Jungle Gardens

Since the early 1930's, Sarasota Jungle Gardens has showcased the flora, fauna and fun of old Florida. This 10 acre site located along the northern bayfront area of the county was originally created to display thousands of tropical plants, trees and flowers from all over the world. Today, these include the rare Australian Nut Tree, a Bunya Bunya tree, the largest Norfolk Island Pine in Florida, Royal Palms, Peruvian Apple Cactus and many native species flourishing in harmony with the exotic transplants. The Gardens are home to a large variety of birds and animals. Visitors can enjoy pink flamingos, parrots, crocodiles, lemurs, snakes and many other critters. Sarasota Jungle Gardens entertains guests with daily educational bird and reptile shows, a Summer Zoo camp, and multiple events throughout the year.

Spring Training

The Sarasota Spring Training tradition began in 1924 when the New York Giants first played at Payne Park. In the years since, many teams have benefited from our perfect spring training weather. Sarasota has been the spring training grounds for the Boston Red Sox, Los Angeles Dodgers, Chicago White Sox and the Cincinnati Reds. Currently the Baltimore Orioles call Ed Smith Stadium their spring home. Twin Lakes Park a county owned 123-acre ballpark also serves as a training base for minor and major league baseball. Twin Lakes consists of 11 baseball fields. Its facilities are available for rental and are utilized by local youth teams and the Sarasota Little League. Over the years the Royals, Mets, Twins, Indians, Reds, Dodgers and Orioles have trained at Twin Lakes Park.

**Courtesy of: Todd Olszewski Team Photographer
for the Baltimore Orioles**

Rowing

Our year-round warm temperatures and calm pristine waterways make the Suncoast the perfect environment for the sport of rowing. Multiple rowing clubs in the area attest to the sport's popularity. Among our clubs are the Sarasota County Rowing Club with 100 adult members, Sarasota Crew offering freshman–varsity youth programs, and the

Sarasota Scullers offering middle and high school student programs. The new Nathan Benderson Park is conveniently located just west of I75 between University Parkway and Fruitville Road, this 600-acre community park with a 500-acre lake provides the ideal location for a multitude of recreational pursuits. Nathan Benderson Park is home to a range of international championships as well as a host of recreational activities including the dragon boat races, canoe and kayak races to triathlon and cross-country events, 5 and 10k runs, wakeboarding, corporate events and much more.

Courtesy of: Sarasota Crew

Polo

Known as "The Sport of Kings," polo has entertained crowds for ages. But, this exciting sport only joined the Suncoast scene in 1991. Sarasota Polo Club hosts matches on *Polo Sundays* throughout the winter months (December – April). These matches are just part of the fun. The Club also offers pony and Clydesdale wagon rides, tailgating, half-time entertainment, and divot stomping. The 130-acre polo grounds are located in Lakewood Ranch, east of Interstate 75 on the south side of University Parkway. For the brave, lessons and arena polo are also available.

Courtesy of: CMS Photography

Fitness

Sarasota features every major gym chain and a large selection of specialized local clubs. You can pursue all the hot workout trends from motion riding spin classes to boxing, MMA training, bootcamps, yoga, ballet bar, pole dancing, and TRX. You can find just the right facility ready to sign you up.

If you are worried about your health as you begin your wellness journey, Sarasota Memorial has a center called HealthFit, which is a medically-oriented fitness center.

As a certified spin, group fitness and TRX trainer, my advice is to research the amenities and class schedules before signing up and try the facility for a month before you commit. You'll find it easy to select a workout facility near where you work or live.

Even if you aren't a gym person, you may be enticed by the Ringling Causeway, which is a sightseers dream for a two mile walk or run. The incline of the bridge provides a nice challenge and is one mile from stoplight to stoplight. Running in the beach sand and swimming in the

Gulf also provide enjoyable outdoor workouts. Whatever your ideal workout, you'll find that the Suncoast has something for everyone.

Getting Fit on the Suncoast

As a Sarasota native and fitness fanatic, I'm delighted to share the array of fun opportunities for fitness within city limits. From water sports to fitness trails, and to great local gyms, your options may seem almost endless.

If you prefer to take in breathtaking views and get up close and personal with local wetlands wildlife, kayaking is a great way to work out your upper body. Sarasota bay hosts some great kayaking spots including the mangrove tunnels located around South Lido Key. You can venture in on your own or take part in a tour hosted by Adventure Kayak Outfitters who provide kayaks to participants.

Paddle boarding pairs a great core workout with the enjoyment of Sarasota's award-winning beaches. Anyone up to the challenge can rent a board and take to the waves of Long Boat Key or Siesta Beach. For those who want a smoother ride, launch a board off the ramps at Bird Key Park. And you'll have lots of company, as it is a popular paddle boarding spot.

If running, walking or biking is more your style, the John Ringling Bridge and the Legacy Trail are for you. The Ringling Bridge, which has a 78.7-foot incline, is great for working your legs and getting some cardio while walking or running the two-mile span. A serious challenge would be riding your bike up the steep incline of this Sarasota landmark against the constant Gulf breeze.

Starting off State Road 72, the Legacy Trail is perfect for bikers and wildlife aficionados. The 10-mile paved trail follows the historic train tracks ending at the refurbished Venice Train Station. Wild animals and strange bugs have been known to cross the path especially then you pass through Oscar Scherer State Park.

When the Florida heat gets to be too much, you can always take your fitness activities to local gyms. Sarasota's array of gyms include specialties such as yoga, dance, and boxing.

Yoga is a tried and true method of increasing flexibility, stamina and overall health. And, there are many studios in the Sarasota area. If the downward dog isn't your thing, take advantage of the wide variety of group fitness classes offered at the dozens of fitness centers throughout the area. Check out a spinning, Zumba or aqua fitness class for a new challenge.

Of course, hiring a personal trainer ensures a great workout specifically catered to you and your needs. Finding a trainer that fits you is a must; some people need a gentle approach while others prefer a serious butt kicking.

Getting fit and staying fit in Sarasota is as easy as finding the right activity for you. With the many options that Sarasota offers, sitting idle should only happen while you're rehydrating.

Derek Flaim is a Certified Personal Trainer and Amateur Boxer who helps Sarasotans meet their fitness goals. Check him out at FlaimFitness.com or reach him at Flaimfitness@gmail.com

Enjoying the Waterways

Boating

Whether you prefer a relaxing sunset cruise aboard a deck boat, offshore fishing on a big rig or paddling your way to a scenic workout, the gentle waters of the Suncoast offer endless recreational opportunities. The Sarasota County Government website supplies a list of area boat launches as well as a Paddle Sarasota map with detailed information on twelve suggested paddling trails. This educational guide provides detailed directions to launch points and information about the adventurous routes.

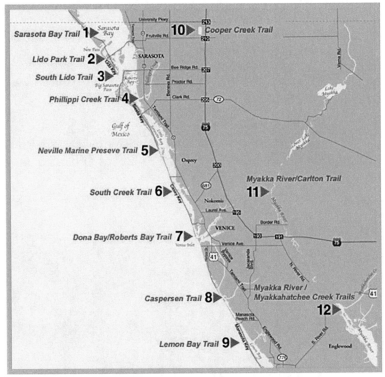

Source: Sarasota County Government www.scgov.net

If you're a newbie to motor or jet powered boating, water safety classes are available through the Sarasota Power & Sail Squadron and the U.S. Coast Guard Auxiliary.

You have three options for obtaining watercraft: Rental, purchase or joining a boating club. Multiple boat rental services are located throughout the area. Until you're sure about your boating commitment, this is an appealing pay as you go option. You don't incur storage or maintenance fees and aren't stuck with a boat you no longer enjoy.

Purchasing a boat is another option and requires registration with the county. You'll also need a place to store and maintain your boat. Your options include:

- Trailering your vessel and launching at a local boat ramp (make sure your homeowners association allows the storage of trailers/boats before undergoing this option)

- Dry storage facilities where the vessel is placed on a rack within a covered building or open space

- Dockage either in a marina or if you are lucky enough in your own backyard

- Joining a boat club such as <u>Freedom Boat Club</u> or <u>Waves Boat Club</u> which market different level memberships that allow you to reserve and utilize a selection of boats to meet your needs

Courtesy of: CMS Photography

Fishing

Abundant fishing enticed the original Northern settlers to our coastal colony. The Gulf of Mexico, coastal bay areas, lakes, Myakka River, creeks and streams are home to approximately 1000 species of fish and sea life.

Mote Marine Laboratory is an excellent learning center about of marine life. With seven research centers, an education division, and the public Mote Aquarium, you'll get answers to all your aquatic questions.

When it comes to catching fish, you can choose your adventure from offshore deep sea trolling, fly fishing, shallow flats casting, and bridge fishing or wading along the shoreline.

Sarasota County has created many man-made reefs to support the growth and health of our fish population. This is terrific for both fisherman and the fish. A complete list of Artificial Reefs is available in the index section. Take your adventure into the water, cast your net and see what underwater treasures are waiting for you to discover.

Whatever type of fishing you choose, you will need a fishing license from the Sarasota County Tax Collector whose website provides a complete list of licensing locations. (It's listed in the index section). To keep our resources healthy and plentiful there are limits to the number and size of fish you can keep. You can find the most current rules and regulations on the Sarasota County Tax Collector's website.

To get help exploring the bays and Gulf of Mexico, you can select from a host of fishing charters available for hire.

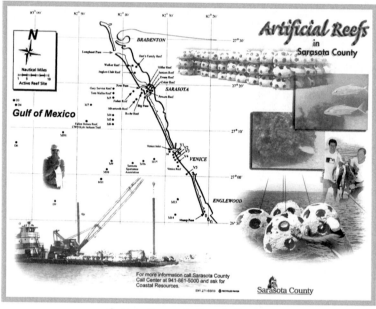

Source: Sarasota County Government www.scgov.net

CHAPTER 7

BRINGING UP BABY & BEYOND-PRE-K TO MBA

We provide wonderful learning experiences for all ages.

Raising children or entertaining grandchildren on the Suncoast is a delightful experience. We are blessed with excellent education choices and year round outdoor activities. We also offer excellent college, graduate, medical school, and adult learning options.

Infant & Toddler Care

For working parents or those who need a much-needed break, Sarasota offers a wide range of daycare options. Private independently-owned facilities, faith-based programs and government-assisted services are widely available throughout the county. _Look for the Stars Quality Improvement System in Sarasota County_ is a tool for parents with children ages 0 to 5 to identify high quality early childcare and education programs and to guide parents in the decision-making process. Their informative website is www.lookforthestars.org/home. html. There are hundreds of childcare options in Sarasota for your little ones. Research what is best for your childcare needs. You can start your investigation at childcarecenter.us, which has narrowed the selection to 127 facilities providing information such as address, size and licensing information. Another option is the Sarasota County childcare referral agency administered by the Early Learning Coalition of Sarasota. Their phone number is 941-556-1600 and their website is http://www.earlylearningcoalitionsarasota.org/. They offer a customized listing of childcare sites and community resources as well as information on scholarships for those in need.

Because turning over the care of your special bundle of joy can be a stressful decision, parents will want to evaluate choices carefully and to make personal visits to the daycare centers. Also, evaluate current customer recommendations before committing.

Our best facilities are in high demand. In fact, many of these popular facilities have waiting lists. So, if you know in advance that you will be moving to Sarasota, do your careful research and secure a place for your children as early as possible. Hiring a babysitter or nanny is another popular option but is often more costly. Two websites can assist you with their helpful recommendations, Care.com and Sittercity.com.

Voluntary Pre-K Programs

To assure that your child has a great induction into the school system, the state of Florida introduced the Voluntary Pre-Kindergarten Program (VPK). This innovative program was created by the state to prepare every four-year–old for a successful kindergarten experience. Vouchers for four-year-olds are also available and accepted by accredited daycare facilities to assist in covering costs for equivalent VPK programs as part of your child's day at the facility. For complete program information visit the Early Learning Coalition of Sarasota County website.

K-12 Education Choices

The Sarasota community delivers a rich and robust learning environment for children including private, public and charter school options available. Sarasota County Schools ranked second in student performance of 67 Florida school districts in 2014, as well as being recognized for "Outstanding Arts Education" by the John F. Kennedy Center for the Performing Arts and the National School Board Associations.

School Name	Type	Charter	Grade 2014	Grade 2013
Alta Vista Elementary School	01	No	A	A
Ashton Elementary School	04	No	A	A
Atwater Elementary	02	No	C	B
Bay Haven School of Basics Plus	03	No	A	A
Booker High School	01	No	B	B
Booker Middle School	03	Yes	C	C
Brentwood Elementary School	04	Yes	B	B
Brookside Middle School	02	Yes	B	A
Cranberry Elementary School	02	No	A	B
Emma E. Booker Elementary School	03	No	C	C
Englewood Elementary School	04	Yes	A	A
Fruitville Elementary School	01	Yes	A	A
Garden Elementary School	01	No	A	B
Glenallen Elementary School	02	No	A	B
Gocio Elementary School	04	Yes	C	C
Gulf Gate Elementary School	04	Yes	A	B
Heron Creek Middle School	02	Yes	C	B
Imagine School at North Port	02	No	A	B
Imagine School At Palmer Ranch	04	Yes	A	A
Island Village Montessori School	01	No	A	A
Lakeview Elementary School	01	No	A	A
Lamarque Elementary School	02	No	C	B
Laurel Nokomis School	01	No	A	A

School Name	Type	Charter	Grade 2014	Grade 2013
North Port High School	01	No	B	B
Pine View School	01	No	A	A
Riverview High School	03	No	A	B
Sarasota Academy of the Arts	01	No	C	
Sarasota High school	01	No	B	B
Sarasota Middle School	01	No	A	A
Sarasota Military Academy	01	No	A	A
Sarasota School of Arts/Sciences	01	No	A	A
Sarasota Suncoast Academy	02	No	B	A
Sky Academy	01	No	C	B
Southside Elementary School	01	No	A	A
Student Leadership Academy	01	No	A	A
Suncoast Polytechnical High School	01	No	A	A
Tatum Ridge Elementary School	01	No	A	A
Taylor Ranch Elementary School	01	No	A	A
Toledo Blade Elementary School	03	No	B	B
Tuttle Elementary School	02	No	A	A
Venice Elementary School	01	No	A	A
Venice Middle School	01	No	A	B
Venice Senior High School	02	No	A	B
Wilkinson Elementary School	03	No	C	B
Woodland Middle School	03	No	B	A

Visit www.sarasotacountyschools.net for complete information

Sarasota County Schools

The Sarasota County School District is ranked second in the state in student achievement. It is one of only 10 of the state's 67 school districts graded as an A district in 2014 by the Florida Department of Education. Residents have supported excellence in public education through additional voted school funding since 2002.

A 2012 independent study by MGT of America concluded that the district is one of the best-run school systems the company has reviewed, citing high performance and innovative practices.

The district is home to 52 schools, including 39 traditional public schools, 12 charter schools and 1 alternative school. Approximately 42,000 students attend Sarasota County schools. Standardized test scores consistently exceed state and national averages.

The district offers school choice and magnet programs, including International Baccalaureate, Advanced International Certificate of Education, two Visual and Performing Arts magnet schools and a technology-focused magnet high school.

TechActive classrooms in middle schools and Technology Enhanced Learning studios in high schools use innovative teaching and state-of-the-art technology to encourage collaborative learning and creative problem solving in a variety of subjects. Career and Technical Education classes prepare students for higher education and the 21st century workforce. High school students can earn college credit, industry certification and the Florida Ready to Work credential.

Full-time programs for intellectually gifted and advanced students are offered throughout the district and at Pine View, a school for gifted students in grades two through 12. In 2013 Pine View was ranked the sixth-best high school in the nation by U.S. News & World Report.

The district has been recognized for outstanding arts education by the John F. Kennedy Center for the Performing Arts and the National School Boards Association. Sarasota is the sixth school district in the U.S. to partner with the Kennedy Center on Any Given Child, a program that works with schools to create a long-range arts education plan for all students.

Twenty-two district schools have received the state Five Star Award for exemplary community involvement. More than 10,000 students, parents, community members and business leaders participate in the district's volunteer program. Team Up!, a web-based resource at TeamUpSCS.org, makes it easy for individuals and businesses to partner with and support their Sarasota County public schools.

Sarasota County Schools

Very bright and high-achieving students can choose from multiple educational options. Pine View School, for students from second grade through twelfth, operates an advanced program designed to meet the distinctive needs of intellectually gifted students. Children are admitted based on a series of tests, recommendations and other relevant data as required by the State Department of Education.

International Baccalaureate (IB) Diploma Programs are also available at multiple public schools within the county. The IB program is a rigorous pre-university course of study leading to internationally standardized tests. Students completing IB courses and exams are eligible for college credits. In our area the following schools have IB programs in place: Brookside Middle School, Phillippi Shores IB World School and Riverview High School.

Currently in Sarasota County there are eleven charter schools: Imagine North Port, Imagine Palmer Ranch, Island Village Montessori Venice, Island Village Montessori Sarasota, Sarasota Academy of the arts, Sarasota Military Academy, Sarasota School of Arts & Sciences, Sarasota Suncoast Academy, Sky Academy, Student Leadership

Academy and Suncoast School for Innovation Studies. Charter schools are tax funded schools that are overseen by the Sarasota County Schools system, although they function largely independently under the terms of their independent contract or district. There is no charge for students to attend a charter school within the district. But, the charter schools do have control over their student population and can target students within a specific age group, grade level, academic level and/or artistic eligibility standards established by the charter school.

There are 39 private school options in Sarasota County currently serving 5936 students. These include parochial schools as well as general studies programs, including schools such as the Julie Rohr Academy, Out of Door Academy, The Achievement Center, New Gate Montessori School, Sarasota Waldorf School and Sea of Strengths Academy. The Out-of-Door Academy services students from Pre-Kindergarten through twelfth grades. The school continues to receive great reviews due to the average student-teacher ratio is 10-1, focusing on boosting the individual student's potential.

Knowing that you have superb K-12 learning options throughout the county should provide real comfort. In fact, according to FloridaTrend. com, 76% of Sarasota County schools meet high standards in reading, 82% in math and 89% in writing. The district has received an A grade from the state every year since 2004 —one of only 13 counties to do so."

Fun Activities for Young Ones

Our abundant art and cultural activities are for children, too. We have plenty to keep them busy and involved. No matter where your child's interests and talents may lead them, you can find a local platform to help them explore them.

Many of the acclaimed art and performance facilities including the Sarasota Ballet, Van Wezel Performing Arts Hall, and Sarasota Orchestra offer youth outreach and educational programs to help develop your child's maximum potential.

With miles of white sandy beaches and heaps of playground filled parks you'll find lots of outdoor activities to tire out your energetic tikes. The Children's Rainforest Garden at Marie Selby Botanical garden complex is currently under construction and will be a wonderful learning adventure for nature loving little ones. To keep them cool in the heat, take a refreshing splash at the Children's Fountain located at Bay Front Park downtown. This fantastic waterpark is fun for children and adults of all ages. Sun-N-Fun is much more than a popular RV campground. It boasts a large recreational facility with a huge pool, a bar and grill, and the super "Hippo" waterslide. Sun-N-fun memberships and day passes are worth every penny. Sarasota has three YMCA facilities offering a variety of adolescent and youth athletic programs. Their websites provide complete information on all of the available youth sports schedules--from tennis to basketball and even tumbling. The Evalyn Sadlier Jones Branch YMCA in Palmer Ranch is home to the Josephine Lofino Splash Park, as well as the Sarasota YMCA Sharks swimming program.

The Boy's & Girls Club of America is another option to assist in getting your child involved in group sports and fun activities. There are three clubs operating within the area. And, don't forget about the Cub, Boy and Girl Scouts organizations all actively engaging the youth in our region.

Keeping Kids Busy on the Suncoast

So much of what there is to see, do and experience in Sarasota is family friendly, making it that much easier to take your kids along for the ride. That includes the sand and surf—and so much more. So go on, don't be afraid to grab your keys, purse (or diaper bag, if they are little) – and let's go!

Since I've already mentioned the sand and surf, I cannot go without talking about the amazing beaches in Sarasota County. In fact, they literally are among the best in the world. If you want some action, check out Siesta Beach on Siesta Key. If you want something a little quieter, try Caspersen Beach, which is known for being a great spot to hunt for fossilized sharks teeth. While you are outside, linger awhile with the kids and grab a kayak to explore the amazingly peaceful mangrove tunnels on Lido. Or head to one of our State Parks, such as Myakka State Park, or Oscar Scherer where you can hike, canoe – or even pitch a tent and camp!

The Ringling Museum is another amazing must experience spot for kids. This 66 acre campus houses world class art, but also the world largest miniature circus, and a hands on spot for kids to attempt a variety of circus stunts, including walking a high wire. (Don't worry, it is only a few inches off the ground.) Other cannot miss spots include Mote Aquarium (say "hi" to Hugh and Buffett, the resident manatee's) and Selby Garden's where kids can explore Florida's flora and fauna!

If you have a budding creative genius on your hands, be sure to check out the offerings from the Sarasota Ballet, Sarasota Opera, Sarasota Orchestra, or Asolo Repertory Theatre. They often have offerings specifically geared towards children. Florida Studio Theatre and Circus Sarasota are additional ones to explore. They often offer unique camps in which children can immerse themselves.

Courtesy of: Jessica Hays

Many area parks are also not to be missed. To celebrate our areas unique circus heritage, Downtown Sarasota is home to an amazingly fun playground at Payne Park. And, your young ones will adore the "cool" playground near Marina Jack's on the bayfront with a sea life inspired fountain play area for your kids to splash around in.

If you're wondering about kid-friendly events, check out visitsarasota.org for an up to date calendar listing of all there is to see and do. I hope your kids enjoy exploring this treasure trove of a community as much as mine do.

Erin Duggan is a Wife & Mother to two boys, Director of Brand for Visit Sarasota County, and overall experience seeker.

If you're looking for activities that both you and your kids can enjoy together, wheel over to the Stardust Skate Center for a spin on the roller rink, or swing by Evie's to practice your short game with an afternoon of miniature golf. The Livingston's Amusement Center is another exhilarating option with a high-speed go cart track, rock climbing wall and arcade games galore.

For an educational option, explore Mote Marine Laboratory or, check out what is happening at one of the seven public libraries conveniently located throughout the County.

College and University Choices

Students of all ages have a broad range of educational opportunities right here on the Suncoast, from attending the nationally recognized New College of Florida, to developing their artistic talents at the Ringling College of Art and Design, or to obtaining a technical certification to jump right into the workforce. New College of Florida has earned many accolades including recognition by Kiplinger's Personal Finance magazine as the seventh best value in public higher education. Time and Money Magazine both named Sarasota's New College as the "2nd Best College Bargain in the Country." New College outranked such schools as the University of California, Berkeley and the University of North Carolina, Chapel Hill. The school considers itself an Honor College with more than 40 majors or "areas of concentration" without grades. Students receive narrative evaluations consisting of useful and informative feedback.

Ringling College of Art & Design is a private four-year college concentrating on fields within the realm of art and design. Majors include Advertising Design, Business of Art & Design, Computer Animation, Digital Filmmaking, General Fine Arts, Graphic Design, Game Art & Design, Graphic Design, Illustration, Interior Design, Motion Design, Sculpture, Painting, Photography & Digital Imaging, and Printmaking. The Ringling College of Art & Design is ranked among the top ten visual and design schools in the county.

Florida State University's College of Medicine and its Film School and are located on the Suncoast.

The Sarasota Regional Medical School Campus provides third and fourth year students the opportunity to complete their hands-on clinical training with local physicians, ambulatory care facilities, and hospitals. Students take part in rotations within the areas of family medicine, internal medicine, pediatrics, surgery, obstetrics-gynecology, geriatrics, psychiatry and emergency medicine.

The FSU/Asolo Conservatory for Actor Training is a three-year graduate program culminating in a Master of Fine Arts degree only available to a select twelve students a year.

State College of Florida Manatee-Sarasota is the region's largest public college serving students on campuses in Bradenton, Lakewood Ranch and Venice as well as offering students learning opportunities through on-campus or online programs. State College of Florida offers Associate and Bachelor degree programs as well as trade certifications to scholars in our area.

University of South Florida at Sarasota-Manatee (USF) located just north of the Sarasota Bradenton International Airport this campus serves both counties and is one of the fastest growing in the USF system. A new campus in North Port reaches southern county students. USF provides students with courses at both the undergraduate and graduate level via traditional classroom learning, E-Learning and video conference technologies.

Suncoast Technical College is accredited by the Commission of the Council on Occupational Education (COE) and the Southern Association of Colleges and Schools (SACS). Suncoast Technical College is divided into four divisions that include, Career & Technical Education (CTE), Sarasota Virtual Academy (SVA) and Suncoast Polytechnic High School (SPHS). The mission of Suncoast Technical College is to provide quality technical education to meet workforce development and community needs. They offer 39 training programs including areas of study in Automotive & Marine Technologies, Business Technologies, Child Care Centers, computer Information Technology, Cosmetology Careers, Criminal Justice Academy, digital & web Design, Drafting, Emergency Medical Services, Fire Service Academy, Health Science, Introduction to HVAC, Precision Machining, Restaurant & Food Services, Suncoast Public Works Academy, and Veterinary Assisting. These courses are available to both adults and high school students to attain college credits or technical program certificates.

Adult Education – Non-Degree Programs

Adult & Community Enrichment (ACE) at STC offers non-credit classes through the School Board of Sarasota County. Classes are offered in a variety of location including the STC campus, Gocio Elementary, The Friendship Center, Whole Foods Market, and the YMCA.

You can select from a wide variety of classes including computer, language, culinary, arts, literature, sports, crafts, and much more. New courses are added to match residents' changing interests. The ACE calendar and program schedule are available online and can also be mailed to you prior to each new semester.

Looking After Your Furry or Feathered Family Members

If you have children of the furry or feathered persuasion, you'll be glad to learn that we have a wonderful Suncoast pet scene.

As a mother to a menagerie of furry children, I am delighted to inform future residents that the veterinarian community in Sarasota is knowledgeable and compassionate. According to Yellowpages.com there are over 220 veterinarians listed in Sarasota County, giving you a plethora of healthcare choices including species specialist and holistic alternatives. You won't have a problem finding an animal clinic near your home for easy pet travel or in case of an emergency. Neighboring pet owners will be your best source for references and experience stories, which will assist in narrowing down the veterinarian selection.

Within the area, we have three "paw" parks in addition to the Venice dog beach. (See our website for the complete list of parks including paw park locations.) Many of our outdoor dining establishments are dog friendly and welcome your canines.

For residents who work full-time, need a break or have a social dog of any size, species or activity level check out Poochie's Pampered Pups, they are a cage-free dog day care and grooming facility. Our Josie attends Poochie's a few days a week and loves having fun with her fellow four-legged friends and always comes home tuckered out from a day of play.

Throughout the year many fundraisers and awareness events benefit our four-legged friends, including: The Pug Parade, Paws on Parade, Santa Paws and the annual Mutt Derby at the Sarasota Kennel Club. We also have Sandy Lane Pet Cemetery and All Pets Memorial Gardens offering honorable burial solutions for your treasured loved ones.

Get Involved in the Community

Associations & Social Ties

Sarasota is a benevolent community, with a billion dollar philanthropic scene that employs more than 5,000 people. We have at least 1545 not-for-profit organizations. To get involved, simply select a charitable cause that is near and dear to your heart and jump right in.

Whether it's the arts, education, children, elderly, animal services, health related issues, we have a dedicated charity that you can help to fulfill their mission. In Sarasota County, two foundations provide leadership and support for not-for-profit organizations: The Community Foundation of Sarasota and Gulf Coast Community Foundation. The Giving Partner can also assist in your exploration of non-profits; this central hub of information contains detailed profiles of registered organizations in the area. The Senior Friendship Center is a resource for seniors looking to get involved. The Friendship Centers organize activities, classes, and volunteer programs to keep seniors actively engaged in the community.

If you would like to join a group of peers for both social and philanthropic reasons, you have plenty of choices. There are organizations in Sarasota to fit everyone's likes or needs from your child's PTA, mom/dad groups, knitting circles, Sarasota Garden Club, becoming a docent at The Ringling Museum, helping with the Southeastern Guide Dogs, Elk's Club, Rotary, Veteran's organizations, sports leagues, church groups. In my own case, as a Junior League of Sarasota member for over ten years, I've been fortunate in having built great relationships through my League experience and to have taken part in many community projects.

The Suncoast Super Boat Grand Prix Festival has taken place for over 29 years and is centered around the offshore powerboat race and includes 15 different events within a nine day period. The funds raised benefit Suncoast Charities for Children.

Visit the Volunteer Sarasota County page on the www.scgov.net website or Volunteer Community Connections for volunteer opportunities.

GULF COAST
COMMUNITY FOUNDATION

The Foundation of Community

Sarasotans love to give. The culture of philanthropy here is as vibrant as the natural beauty, artistic creativity, and cosmopolitan air that draw so many here in the first place. And while the legacy of giving in this community is long, some of our biggest philanthropists are relative newcomers too.

Fortunately, those aspiring philanthropists can benefit from the expertise of Gulf Coast Community Foundation, which has been transforming our region through bold and proactive philanthropy since 1995. A partner for local nonprofits and a steward for donors who want to enhance this community, Gulf Coast is best known for creating strategic initiatives that will move our community forward—and engaging community members of all means in bringing them to life.

Gulf Coast's STEMsmart project has gained national attention for improving science and math education in Sarasota County middle and high schools. The technology-friendly STEMsmart "Classrooms of Tomorrow" have become a major draw for students—who often don't want to leave when their class period ends! Gulf Coast also provides vital support to the arts institutions that color our cultural life and the environmental groups that preserve Sarasota's coastal treasures. Through the foundation's GulfCoastGood.org website, "citizen philanthropists" can find great charity projects and volunteer opportunities in their own backyard—a great way to get to know this community.

Most important, the foundation educates donors about the greatest opportunities and challenges facing our community and then connects them with ways to make a bigger difference through their giving than they ever could on their own.

Everything Gulf Coast does is for the good of this community. The foundation's committed, generous donors exemplify a favorite phrase of the organization: "to donate" begins with "to do." Whether you have just arrived or are planning your move here, I invite you to contact Gulf Coast Community Foundation to learn how you can get meaningfully involved in your new hometown.

Michael Saunders is on the Board of Directors for Gulf Coast Community Foundation, and Founder and CEO of Michael Saunders & Company.

You'll find it's easy to keep up with what's happening on the scene. At least three local magazines, multiple newspapers, and many websites cover every event in Sarasota. Sarasota Magazine, SRQ Magazine, Scene Magazine, and The Observer Group do a fantastic job enlightening you on the who, what, when and where of our bustling town. Events are also published each Thursday in The Sarasota Herald Tribune Ticket section of the newspaper.

So, get out and get active.

The Suncoast Social and Volunteer Scene

The Suncoast has an extremely welcoming and inclusive social environment. You will be able to find your community volunteer niche quite easily as long as you are willing to work hard and/ or give to a cause. Most importantly, find something you care about.

During "Season", the precious months between October and May, you can attend a black-tie charity gala every weekend, if you choose. There is an entire mini-

Courtesy of: Debbi Benedict

industry built around charitable events in Sarasota. Certain weeks during Season there is a charitable luncheon almost every day.

Dozens of charities need your help – everything from battered women, to at-risk children, to health-related issues, to the many cultural and performing arts organizations, to animals in need and many, many more. How to choose? If you're working, what does your employer support? That is always a good starting place. Women might want to consider the Junior League of Sarasota which can be a springboard to serving on committees and boards across the city.

Let's not forget your child's school, your church or synagogue, or your neighborhood country club. All figure very prominently in our social scene. We have several outstanding private and public schools, many popular events supporting Jewish and Catholic causes, and there are lots of country clubs scattered throughout the area, some more chi-chi than others, of course.

Another terrific way to see where you might be a good fit is to study the social pages and society photos. Sarasota is blessed with all manner of society event coverage starting with the local daily newspaper, The Herald Tribune, and the weekly Observer. We also have several glossy magazines that feature a myriad of photos with stunningly dressed men and women as well as those Sarasotans who prefer to give back with a more hands-on form of volunteerism.

You may love black tie events or hate them. You may love swinging a hammer at Habitat for Humanity or prefer managing a charity auction. Whatever your preference, we are waiting for you with open arms!

Debbi Benedict, SCENE Magazine's society maven and lifestyle blogger at www.thecivilizedlifeinsarasota.blogspot.com.

If you are currently focused on your career or on building your own business, you will find great networking groups related to your professional focus. The Greater Sarasota Chamber of Commerce, as well as some of the smaller community Chambers are a fantastic resource for getting involved. The Sarasota Chamber also organizes a thriving Young Professional Group (YPG). Leadership Sarasota, also offered through the Chamber, is a leadership program designed to nurture and engage current and future leaders by teaching them "how things work" in our community and our country.

Local Media: TV, Radio, Print, Online

Sarasota local news, traffic and weather are on:

- SNN – Channel 6 News

- WFLA-TV - Channel 8 – NBC, Tampa

- WFTS – Channel 28 – ABC, Tampa

- WTSP – Channel 10 – CBS, Tampa

- WTVT – Channel 13 – FOX, Tampa

- WVEA – Channel 62 – Univision

- WWSB - Channel 40 – ABC

*** The cable or satellite provider you chose will determine your local and national channel numbers. Sarasota News Now (SNN) is a continual news channel that is owned and operated by the Sarasota Herald Tribune. This channel may not be available from all providers. The Tampa network stations include Sarasota in their local weather, traffic and news coverage providing multiple channel options.

Sarasota's Strongest FM Radio Stations:

- 88.1 FM – WJIS Religious

- 89.1 FM – WSMR Classical

- 89.7 FM – WUSF Talk

- 90.5 FM – WBVM Religious

- 92.1 FM - WDDV Adult contemporary

- 92.9 FM – WIKX Country

- 93.3 FM – WFLZ Top 40

- 94.1 FM – WSJT Smooth jazz

- 94.9 FM – WWRM Adult contemporary

- 98.7 FM – WLLD Top 40

- 99.5 FM - WQYK Country

- 100.7 FM - WMTX Top 40

- 101.5 FM - WPOI Top 40

- 102.5 FM – WHPT Talk

- 103.5 FM - WTBT Country

- 104.3 FM – WKZM Religious/talk

- 104.7 FM – WRBQ Classic hits

- 105.9 FM – WTZB Top 40

- 106.5 FM - WCTQ Country

- 107.9 FM – WSRZ Oldies/classics

Sarasota's Strongest AM Radio Stations:

- 540 AM – WFLA Talk

- 740 AM – WQTM Sports/talk

- 820 AM – WMGG News/talk

- 930 AM – WLSS Talk radio

- 970 AM – WFLA News/talk

- 1010 AM – WQYK Sports/talk

- <u>1110 AM</u> – WTIS Christian

- <u>1220 AM</u> - WIBQ Talk

- <u>1250 AM</u> - WHNZ News/talk

- <u>1280 AM</u> – WTMY Sports

- <u>1320 AM</u> – WAMR Oldies/nostalgia

- <u>1420 AM</u> – WBRD Regional Mexican

- <u>1450 AM</u> - WSRQ Talk

*** Programming subject to change at discretion of independent stations

Print Newspapers:

Our local daily newspapers are <u>The Herald Tribune</u> and the <u>Venice Herald Tribune</u>. The biweekly <u>Venice Gondolier Sun</u> is published on Wednesday and Sundays. <u>The Observer Group</u> publishes regionally targeted papers including The East County Observer, The Sarasota Observer, The Longboat Observer, and The Pelican Press, all of which are printed weekly on Thursdays.

Local Magazines:

- <u>BIZ941</u>
- <u>Edible Sarasota</u>
- <u>Florida Family Living</u>
- <u>Florida Homes Magazine</u>
- <u>Golf Coast Magazine</u>
- <u>Natural Awakenings</u>
- <u>Real Magazine</u>
- <u>Sarasota Magazine</u>
- <u>Sarasota Mommy Magazine</u>
- <u>Scene Magazine</u>
- <u>SRQ Magazine</u>

CHAPTER 8
PRACTICAL NOTEBOOK ON MOVING

Moving Calendar

The best time of year to make the move to Sarasota depends on many factors. If you're being relocated, you may not control the timing. But, if you can choose, you may want to opt for the relatively cool and dry November to May months. During the peak Thanksgiving to Easter period, you may find lots of traffic delays.

In terms of the school year, many parents now prefer to move while school is in session so it's easier to make new friends The first and last few days of the month tend to be the busiest moving times, so avoid them. And, holiday schedules might result in unnecessary delays.

Happily, after the journey, hard work and frustration, the rewards of sun-drenched beaches, warm weather, and southern hospitality await you.

Moving Assistance

The thought of packing up all of your belongings and traveling across the country or the globe can be very daunting. There are many ways to manage the rigors of your move, whether you personally pack up your household and rent a truck on your own or hire a company to assist you. To make the move as smooth as possible, here are a few things to consider before you begin:

129

Will my current furniture work/fit into my new Florida home and lifestyle? This is a very important question. Because, before you pay to ship these items to Sarasota, it's wise to determine if they will fit the style and décor of your new home. And, are they the correct scale and size? Our floor plans are more open and our ceilings are typically higher than most northern homes. We also tend to use lighter weight fabrics and colors. Do I need all these winter clothes? Probably not. You won't need to bring a stockpile of winter wear unless you plan frequent trips back to the frozen north. Yes, you will need a few light jackets, some rain boots and maybe a hat or two. Should I bring all my stuff from the basement and attic? Only if you are moving into a very large house. I know of only one historic home in Sarasota that has a basement. Although there may be a few others around, forget the storage luxury of a basement in Sarasota. Unless you buy a huge home with lots of empty rooms or dedicated storage space, consider shrinking your belongings before packing up your current household. Many new residents put rarely used into an offsite storage unit. Of course, many of us wind up giving away everything we placed in storage and never used.

Depending on your situation, you may require the assistance of a national moving company. Of course, you'll want multiple quotes and multiple references for the moving companies you are considering before signing on the dotted line.

Below is a list of national and local moving companies.

National and Local Moving Assistance:

- Allied Van Lines 1-800-444-6787

- Two Men and a Truck 1-877-263-6444

- AAA Flat Rate Moving & Storage 1-800-741-3213

- The Moving Solution, LLC. 1-941-706-4474

- Yarnell 1-941-365-3060

- North American Van Lines 1-800-369-9115

Transportation & Logistics

Getting all of your belongings safely to Sarasota may seem overwhelming. But, a wide range of services exist to assist you.

Car carriers transverse the county delivering vehicles from one location to another without the wear and tear on your car or your person. When calculating the mileage, fuel, tolls, and service required hiring a carrier to deliver your vehicle may be a smarter option. This is also true for transporting boats.

If you are moving to a temporary residence while searching for your perfect home or while your home is under construction, a climate controlled warehouse or storage facility is a must. Air conditioned storage facilities come in many shapes and sizes with options including drive-up access, first floor access and storage rooms located on a higher level floor which require the use of elevators and tight hallways. Rates are relative to convenience and size—and may be a substantial monthly outlay. Therefore careful storage research is essential. To narrow your options in the region the Sparefoot Storage Finder website.

Below is a list of air conditioned storage facilities you may want to consider:

- <u>Bee Ridge Self Storage</u> 941-306-4175

- <u>Cube Smart</u> 1-877-279-0721

- <u>Extra Space Storage</u> 855-676-1555

- <u>Hide-Away Storage</u> 941-755-1166 (corporate number; they have 4 locations)

- <u>Lock Tite Storage</u> 941-923-9595

- <u>Sarasota Self Storage</u> 941-306-4128

CHAPTER 9

THE ECONOMY ON THE REBOUND

Source of Vitality

The Florida economy is expected to outpace the nation in 2015 due to strong employment gains and economic growth according to BMO Economics. "It's good news to see such impressive growth in the Florida economy," said Dave Maraman, the Sarasota-based Florida regional president for business banking at BMO Harris Bank to the Herald Tribune in February of 2015.

BMO's indicators for Southwest Florida economic strength are:

- Increased population numbers

- Economic expansion, real GDP in Florida should grow to 3.3 percent in 2015, up from the 2.7 percent of 2014 and slightly ahead of the national average

- Real estate service employment is recovering quickly

- Construction employment is rising up 9.4 percent year-over-year

- New construction growth Employflorida.com indicates that in November of 2014 our area's unemployment rate was 5.3%, lower than the state average of 5.6% and the national average of 5.8%.

According to Floridatrend.com the top five industry classes for employment in Sarasota are retail trade, healthcare, construction, administrative/waste services, and accommodation/food services. In fact, Sarasota beats the national average for the percentage of jobs in the following fields: Healthcare and social services and leisure and hospitality services. That's not surprising because of our large retirement population and the importance of tourism to our economy.

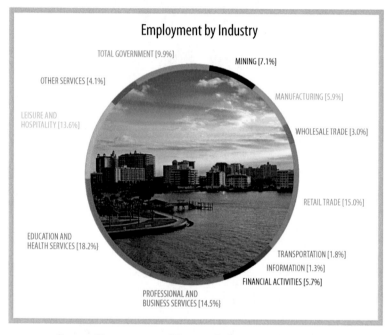

Employment by Industry

TOTAL GOVERNMENT [9.9%]

MINING [7.1%]

OTHER SERVICES [4.1%]

MANUFACTURING [5.9%]

LEISURE AND HOSPITALITY [13.6%]

WHOLESALE TRADE [3.0%]

RETAIL TRADE [15.0%]

EDUCATION AND HEALTH SERVICES [18.2%]

TRANSPORTATION [1.8%]

INFORMATION [1.3%]

FINANCIAL ACTIVITIES [5.7%]

PROFESSIONAL AND BUSINESS SERVICES [14.5%]

Source: Department of Economic Opportuniey, Sept 2014 OCEW

More than 18 percent of the jobs in Sarasota are in the healthcare sector compared to roughly 11 percent nationwide. A task force established by the Economic Development Corporation (EDC) of Sarasota County is researching ways to stimulate "medical tourism" by capitalizing on the regions award winning medical facilities.

Because we boast the Nation's number one beach, related jobs benefit directly. Sarasota County notches an above average 13.6 percent of area jobs in the leisure and hospitality industry compared to the national average of just 10 percent. Our new Nathan Benderson Park is expected to make us an international rowing destination. That bodes well for growing strength in our leisure and tourism numbers, continuing to surpass the national average.

Our arts-intensive Suncoast community generates employment in arts-related companies that's nearly as large of a share of total employment as Manhattan.

In addition, our area's wealth has attracted more than fifty financial institutions, including over a dozen private banks that cater specifically to high net worth clients.

Although the construction industry declined considerably after the housing crash, it has begun to recover and remains a critical jobs provider in our local economy. New home sales are rebounding, which is best demonstrated by the permit chart below from the Sarasota county Planning and Development Services.

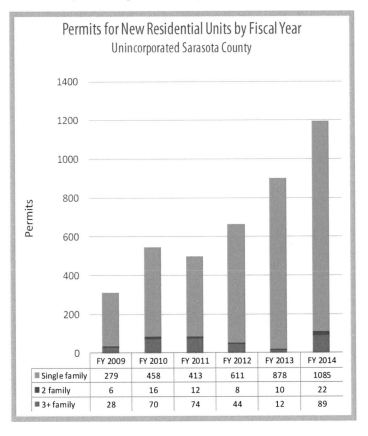

Permits for New Residential Units by Fiscal Year
Unincorporated Sarasota County

	FY 2009	FY 2010	FY 2011	FY 2012	FY 2013	FY 2014
Single family	279	458	413	611	878	1085
2 family	6	16	12	8	10	22
3+ family	28	70	74	44	12	89

Employment Statistics

Rank	Occupation Group	2011 Estimated Employment	2019 Projected Employment
1	Office and Administrative Support Occupations	26,995	30,302
2	Sales and Related Occupations	18,818	21,133
3	Food Preparation and Serving Related Occupations	16,544	18,859
4	Healthcare Practitioners and Technical Occupations	11,139	12,993
5	Construction and Extraction Occupations	7814	9769
6	Building and Grounds Cleaning and Maintenance Occupations	8179	9159
7	Healthcare Support Occupations	6974	8594
8	Business and Financial Operations Occupations	6920	8067
9	Education, Training, and the Library Occupations	6647	7806
10	Installation, Maintenance, and Repair Occupations	6030	6984
11	Personal Care and Service Occupations	5667	6667
12	Management Occupations	5467	6127
13	Transportation and Material Moving Occupations	5393	6072
14	Production Occupations	4826	5261
15	Arts, Design, Entertainment, Sports, and Media Occupations	3181	3581

Source: employflorida.com

Top 10 Private Employers		
Company	Full-Time	Primary Product/Service
PGT Industries	1440	Window and Door Manufacturer
Publix	1335	Grocery Store Chain
Venice Regional Medical Center	1200	Hospital
FCCI Insurance Group	720	Insurance
Sun Hydraulics Corporation	702	Manufacturer-Hydraulic Cartridge Valves
Goodwill Industries	682	Not-for-profit Retailer
Tervis Tumbler	619	Insulated Plastic Tumbler Manuf.
Sunset Automotive Group	650	Automobile Retailer
Doctors Hospital of Sarasota	437	Hospital
Pines for Sarasota	342	Not-for-profit Nursing and Assisted Living Center

Top Government Employers		
Company	Full-time	Primary Product/Service
School Board of Sarasota County	4664	Public Education
Sarasota Memorial Health Care System	3099	Healthcare
Sarasota County	2052	Municipality
Sheriff	976	Municipality
City of Sarasota	596	Municipality
City of North Port	523	Municipality
New College of Florida	255	Public Education
City of Venice	252	Municipality
Clerk of Circuit Court	221	Municipality
USF Sarasota/Manatee	175	Public Education

Note: The Economic Development Corporation of Sarasota County has compiled this listing of the largest private and government employers in Sarasota County based upon information provided. This information may be subject to change. These figures are approximate as of November 2013. Source: www.employflorida.com

Efforts to Diversify the Economy & Support Growth

CNNMoney.com named Sarasota one of the "Top 10 Turnaround Towns" in 2012 and we have remained in a positive recovery mode since then. The area is dominated by small businesses with 80% of companies having fewer than 10 employees. The region also contains a high number of solopreneurs. The City of Sarasota was awarded the Google 2014 eCity Award, Sarasota was determined to have the top online business presence in Florida, connecting with customers and stimulating the digital economy.

Businesses of all sizes can seek advice from multiple resources in the area including the Greater Sarasota Chamber of Commerce, or more community specific chambers (see our website for a complete list of local chambers), Economic Development Corporation (EDC) of Sarasota, SCOPE, the Florida Economic Gardening Institute's Grow Florida program, SCORE, and The HuB.

The Economic Development Corporation (EDC) of Sarasota is a public/private partnership focused on growing and diversifying the local economy. The EDC is a rich resource for businesses that are considering expanding or relocating to Sarasota.

GrowFL is part of the Florida Economic Gardening Institute (FEGI). They encourage growth from local businesses who share the values and objectives of grass root economic pursuits, Main Street initiatives, and focus on sustainability, in addition to local food programs. GrowFL provides support for companies in the initial startup phase or early stages of development.

SCOPE stands for Sarasota County Openly Plans for Excellence. Their mission is to connect and inspire citizens to create a better community. SCOPE offers hi-tech, hi-touch workshops and is currently working on a community data initiative. Their focus is engaging citizens within the community.

SCORE, The Manasota Chapter of SCORE covers Manatee and Sarasota counties in Florida and has over 60 volunteers locally to assist existing and start up companies with education and mentoring on a wide range of business issues.

The HuB is a progressive and successful economic development concept best described by their website, "The HuB is a creative and collaborative space and community where entrepreneurs come together to develop ideas and contribute toward building a new economy and culture." Since their inception in 2009 the HuB has supported over two-hundred entrepreneurs, launched twenty businesses, and twelve major campaigns to support creative change on the Suncoast.

Courtesy of: The HuB

Employment Market

Half of Sarasota County households earn more than $50,000 a year and nearly 30 percent earn more than $75,000 year. In August of 2015 there were 9,208 job openings advertised online in Sarasota County according to employflorida.com.

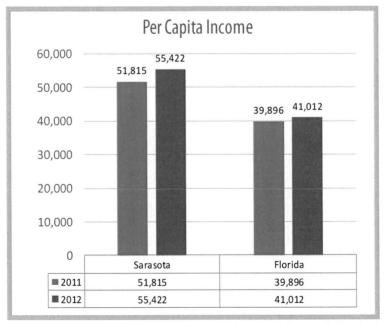

Per Capita Income

	Sarasota	Florida
2011	51,815	39,896
2012	55,422	41,012

Source: U. S. Department of Commerce, Bureau of Economic Analysis

The table below shows the occupations with the highest paying 2014 estimated median (annual) wages in Sarasota County, Florida.

Rank	Occupation	2014 Estimated Median Annual Wage
1	Specializing Physicians	$189,422
2	Chief Executives	$188,650
3	Family & General Practitioners	$183,079
4	Psychiatrists	$174,697
5	Judges	$145,417
6	Dentists, General	$137,144
7	Airline Pilots	$126,524
8	Computer and Information Systems Managers	$123,326
9	Sales Managers	$116,724
10	Pharmacists	$115,926

Source: Employflorida.com Occupation LMI Analyzer August 2015

Notable Companies in the Area (List from FloridaTrend.com):

- **Benderson Development** — Benderson is one of the Sarasota area's biggest developers of shopping centers and commercial space as well as the Nathan Benderson Park.

- **Eco Trans Alliance** — Makes solar tops that transform battery-powered electric low-speed vehicles like golf carts and trams into solar-electric vehicles.

- **FCCI Insurance Group** — Beginning as a workers' comp firm, FCCI has expanded into other lines and now has $1.8 billion in assets and does business in 14 states.

- **IntegraClick** — A privately held firm run by youthful executives offers online marketing services.

- **Ivir** — Designs medical and military modeling and simulation programs and systems.

- **L-3 Communications** — Makes the "black box" (it's actually orange) flight recorders and other instrumentation.

- **Lakewood-Amedex** — Startup genetic technology firm specializes in biopharmaceuticals, with applications in "gene silencing" and treating infectious diseases.

- **LexJet** — Designs, makes and markets wide-format inkjet printing equipment. The company's founders have also started a company, Digital Leather that does custom digital printing on leather.

- **METI** (Medical Education Technologies) — Manufacturer of medical training technology, including patient simulators.

- **Osprey Biotechnics** — Makes bacteria used in industrial, environmental and agricultural applications.

- **PGT Industries** — Door and window manufacturer had to downsize after the real estate collapse but remains a top employer.

- **Robrady Design** — Design and product development firm takes ideas from concept to market.

- **Star2Star Communications** — Makes and markets a business telephone system using voice-over-internet protocol.

- **Sun Hydraulics** — Sun designs and manufactures hydraulic cartridge valves for industrial uses.

- **Sunovia Energy Technologies** — Develops and markets products in the solar technology and LED lighting markets.

- **Tervis Tumbler** — Manufacturer of insulated cups that has had explosive growth under CEO Laura Spencer.

- **Willis A. Smith Construction** — Commercial construction and planning company specializes in green building.

- **Zenith National Insurance** — The workers' comp insurer does business in 45 states.

Sarasota's business and economic climate prove to be recovering from the recession with great strides. The areas low un-employment numbers, increasing permit numbers and escalating population growth are positive signs for continued improvement and success. Sarasotans and have access to brilliant local resources including the EDC, Greater Sarasota Chamber of Commerce and the Hub, supporting business and entrepreneurial pursuits. A great number of inventive and productive companies are thriving along the Suncoast.

CONCLUSION

Sarasota is a culturally rich community with an abundance of intriguing people, fascinating art, and miles of captivating coastline, which offers a lifestyle like no other.

Multiple housing options and a wide variety of communities suit every lifestyle. Affordable living costs enable young families and retirees alike to live well without being wealthy.

A healthy economic atmosphere and low unemployment makes for a sensible place to forge a career, build a business, raise a family, and enjoy an active retirement. That's why it makes so much sense to begin the next chapter of your life right here along our crystal white Suncoast shoreline.

In a dynamic city that is constantly evolving and enhancing its Suncoast treasures, we've done our best to highlight Sarasota's great attractions, people, places or traits. But, as you get settled and begin building your life in our beautiful city, you will undoubtedly make fascinating discoveries all your own. Be sure to let us know about them so we can consider adding them to the second edition.

As you get busy creating the story of your own life, remember to take time to walk the beach, be mesmerized by the sunset, soak your soul in the salty Gulf waters, and smile at your neighbor. After all, living on the Suncoast is only a dream for most people. But, for you, it can be a delightful reality.

I look forward to seeing you out and about as you enjoy all the jewels of Sarasota, the place I am proud to call home.

Isn't it time you moved to Sarasota?

ACKNOWLEDGMENTS

I truly never thought I would be given the opportunity to write a book about the community I so proudly call home.

The saying *"it is not what you know, but who you know"* completely explains how this exciting endeavor came my way. I penned these pages only because my dear friend and Junior League colleague, Erin Duggan, introduced me to Newt Barrett, this book's kind, patient and stellar publisher. Newt's desire to create such a helpful moving guide was inspirational. His complete guidance, thorough editing, and assistance have kept me sane and on track throughout this process.

I must also thank Ed Bertha, owner and publisher of Real Magazine, for giving me my first freelance writing opportunity. I will never forget his faith in my abilities and continued support over the years.

I owe my patient and endearing husband, Jeff, a much-needed vacation with my undivided attention. He distracted me when I appeared blind and blundering. And, he left me alone when I was focused and on a mission. Jeff has graciously eaten his share of unhealthy takeout and folded a few extra loads of laundry to allow me the essential time for research and writing.

A million thanks to my great friends Kimmie, Heather, and Shannon, who have gracefully dealt with my distracted attention and unavailability. To my dear loving father, all I can say is "anyways."

To my supportive work team, the Schemmel Property Group - Joel, Sharon, and Todd-- thank you for not pointing out when I appeared tired or stressed and for supporting my efforts in creating a book that will be beneficial to our community.

For the fantastic photos that are the highlight of this book, I thank:

- Chad Spencer with CMS Photography

- Detlev Von Kessel with pix360

- Robert Pope with Robert Pope Photography

You have all been generous godsends. Your visions through the lens are pure art and have made this book as beautiful as it is useful.

Extreme gratitude goes to:

- Alysia Shivers for leading the way with <u>Moving to Naples</u>, the first of many fantastic Un-Tourist Guides,

- Jamie Ebling for reviewing my writers agreement and making sure that I was not selling any vital organs in the process,

- Jeff LaHurd for the fantastic foreword and historic fact checking.

Many thanks and great appreciation to everyone who assisted me and contributed to this project including:

- Erin Duggan with Visit Sarasota County

- Lorrie Muldowny Manager Sarasota County Historical Resources

- Debbi Benedict with Scene Magazine

- Martha J. Robinson with the Florida Park Service

- Wendy Rose with the Sarasota County Sheriff's Office

- Duval's New World Café

- Michaels On East

- Todd Olszewski Team Photographer for the Baltimore Orioles

- Fern Segerlind Historic Spanish Point

- Sarasota Crew

- Derrick Flaim personal trainer to yours truly

- Michael Saunders and the Gulf Coast Community Foundation

- Mike Marraccini with the Sarasota Ballet

- Kay Rosaire and Richard Czina with Big Cat Habitat and Gulf Coast Sanctuary

- Kelly Munch with Sarasota Memorial Health Care System

- Jane Goodwin and Scott Ferguson with Sarasota County Schools

- Reid Gerletti

- Daniel Volz nightlife expert

- Ed Wisburn Photography

- Scott Guinn with the Sarasota Opera

- Lorry Eible and Lori Ann Steiner of Foxy Lady

Last but not least, I send thanks to my mentor and colleague, Michelle Burke-Phillips, who has always supported me in all my ventures, who has been a strong and passionate figure in my life for over ten years. She continues to be a positive, yet honest source of encouragement. Without your rational opinions, inspirational notes, and warm smiles I would "leap" less often.

AUTHOR BIOGRAPHY

Tracy Eisnaugle enjoyed a successful career as a designer in Sarasota, utilizing her B.S. in Interior Design from F.S.U. Her work history includes high end residential design, model merchandizing, and managing a design center for Lee Wetherington Homes. She began her writing career while taking a break from the design industry. Tracy offered copywriting and marketing services for local real estate professionals, as well as writing feature articles for Real Magazine and Scene Magazine. She now focuses her professional efforts in real estate marketing as the Marketing Coordinator for the Sarasota and Tampa Regions at Premier Sotheby's International Realty.

As a resident of Sarasota for over thirty years Tracy is passionate about the community and its people. Among her community volunteer roles are: Sustaining member of The Junior League of Sarasota, member of The Young Professionals Group, past board member for JOY, volunteer with Habitat for Humanity, and committee member for The New College Library Fund and Children First.

Tracy is happily married to her husband Jeff, a 3rd generation Sarasotan and owner of TJ's Landscaping & Tree service.

KEY RESOURCES: WEBSITES AND PHONE NUMBERS

Go online for our extensive list of Sarasota resources

For the latest information about moving to and living in Sarasota, please visit our companion website: www.movingtosarasotaguide.com

If you need to access our extensive resource page quickly, go directly to: www.movingtosarasotaguide.com/resources

Important Contact Information and website links:

Business Assistance:

Greater Sarasota Chamber of Commerce
941-955-8187
www.sarasotachamber.com

Siesta Key Chamber of Commerce
941-349-3800
www.siestakeychamber.com

North Port Area Chamber of Commerce
941-564-3040
www.northportareachamber.com
Venice Area Chamber of Commerce
941-488-2236
www.venicechamber.com

Longboat Key Chamber of Commerce
941-383-2466
www.longboatkeychamber.com

SCORE
941-955-1029
www.manasota.score.org

Occupational Licensing
Sarasota County Tax Collector
941-861-8300
www.sarasotataxcollector.com
(if you live within a city limit a city business tax may also be applicable)

Cable and Telephone Services:

Comcast
941-371-6700
www.comcast.com

Verizon (fiber optics)
800-483-4000
www.22verizon.com

Utilities and Garbage Collection:

Electric
Florida Power & Light
941-917-0708
www.fpl.com

Gas
TECO Peoples Gas
877-832-6747
www.peoplesgas.com

Recycling & Waste Management:
Garbage Collection (non-city) Sarasota County
941-861-5000
www.scgov.net

North Port Solid Waste
941-240-8050
www.cityofnorthport.com

Sarasota Solid Waste
941-365-7652
www.scgov.net

Waste Management
941-924-1254
www.wm.com

Water & Sewage
City of Sarasota Public Works
941-954-4198
www.sarasota.gov

Education:

School Board of Sarasota County
941-927-9000
www.sarasotacountyschools.net

Emergency/Medical:

In case of an emergency, dial 911

Fire Departments:

Longboat Key 941-316-1944 www.longboatkey.org
Nokomis 941-488-8855 www.nokomisvfd.org
North Port 941-423-4353 www.northportfd.org

Sarasota County 941-861-5300 www.sarasotafire.com
Venice 941-480-3030 www.venicegov.com

Government:

City of North Port
941-429-7000
www.cityofnorthport.com

City of Sarasota
941-356-2200
www.sarasotagov.com

City of Venice
941-486-2626
www.venicegov.com

Town of Longboat Key
941-316-1999
www.longboatkey.org

Sarasota County
941-861-5000
www.scgov.net

Social Security
800-772-1213
www.ssa.gov

Tax Collector

Sarasota County Tax Collector 941-861-8300
www.sarasotataxcollector.com

Hospitals:

Doctors Hospital of Sarasota 941-342-1100 www.doctorsofsarasota.com
Sarasota Memorial Hospital 941-917-9000 www.smh.com
Venice Regional Medical Center 941-485-7711 www.veniceregional.com

Police Non-Emergency:

City of Sarasota 941-366-8000 www.sarasotapd.org
Longboat Key 941-316-1977 www.longboatkey.org
North Port 941-429-7300 www.cityofnorthport.com
Venice 941-486-2444 www.venice.gov

Sheriff Department:

Sarasota County Sheriff 941-861-5800 www.sarasotasheriff.org

Registrations and Licensing:

Driver's License Office
941-361-6222
www.hsmv.state.fla.us

Fishing License
Sarasota County Tax Collector 941-861-8300
www.sarasotataxcollector.com

License Plates, Vehicle & Vessel Registration:
Sarasota County Tax Collector
941-861-8300
www.sarasotataxcollector.com

Transportation:

Air

Sarasota-Bradenton International Airport (SRQ)
941-359-2777
www.srq-airport.com

Venice Municipal Airport (VNC)
941-486-2711
www.venicegov.com

Public

Amtrak
800-872-7245
www.amtrak.com

941-861-1020 or 941-861-1234
www.scgov.net.scat

Sarasota Trolley
941-346-3115
www.sarasotatrolley.com

SRQ Trolley
941-538-1414
www.srqtrolley.com

Roadways
Florida Department of Transportation
www.dot.state.fl.us